MW00784766

*Eagle and shield on a 19th-century presidential
wineglass (see figure 11) give expression
to a youthful country's pride and patriotism.*
COVER: *Detail of the glass above.*

Eagle and shield on a 19th-century presidential wineglass (see figure 11) give expression to a youthful country's pride and patriotism.
COVER: Detail of the glass above.

WHITE HOUSE
Glassware

Two Centuries of Presidential Entertaining

by

Jane Shadel Spillman

Windows aglow, the President's House beckons guests to a reception in
January 1886. Less than six months later, cut and engraved table glassware
added sparkle to the White House wedding reception of
President and Mrs. Grover Cleveland. From the ornate to the
classically simple, glassware of quality has served every administration.

WHITE HOUSE
Glassware
Two Centuries of Presidential Entertaining

by

Jane Shadel Spillman

Curator of American Glass
The Corning Museum of Glass

Published by

The White House Historical Association

in cooperation with

The National Geographic Society and The Corning Museum of Glass

Reflections

The President and I greatly enjoy entertaining at the White House—we love sharing this magnificent place with guests from around the country and from around the world, and we also love sharing it with family and friends. Living with the special treasures chosen so carefully by other presidential families brings us closer to America's past.

The grace of that past can be seen in glassware of quality, used by our country's Presidents and First Ladies since George Washington took office in 1789. These lovely objects help to make each White House dinner and reception a beautiful sight. Holding a White House glass is like holding a piece of history.

Learning more about this history is one of the pleasures and privileges of living in the White House. The China Room holds a display of selected pieces, including a water bottle used by Abraham Lincoln, a wineglass with the coat-of-arms design preferred by Benjamin Harrison, and a decanter purchased by Andrew Jackson. Most of the irreplaceable collection, however, has been stored away for safety's sake.

And now, with the publication of this important book, comes the unprecedented opportunity for a look at some of the rare period pieces from the White House glassware collection. In celebration of this volume, some of the stored objects will be placed on display in the ground-floor corridor. For the first time, every visitor to the White House can share the joy of seeing the historic glassware that belongs to all Americans.

Barbara Bush

Engraved grapevines and grapes garland this 19th-century wineglass from the White House collection (see figure 11).

5

Foreword

When I guided Jane Spillman to the White House storage rooms and showed her the vast quantity of historic glassware housed there, she was astonished at the size and richness of the collection. Although much of the glass has disappeared over the years, either broken or sold at public sales of White House objects, more than 870 pieces of 19th-century American glass have survived in the White House.

From the earliest days of the house, entertaining has been an important duty of the President and his wife or hostess. The White House glassware, like the state china services, has been an essential part of the social and political history of the President's House.

The growth of the White House collections has been paralleled by an increased interest in American decorative arts. These changes, in turn, have created the need for informative publications about the historic objects associated with the White House. Although the porcelain state dinner services already have been thoroughly documented, no comprehensive study of the glass collection has been previously available. We in the Office of the Curator of the White House are very pleased that Jane Shadel Spillman, curator of American glass at The Corning Museum of Glass, agreed to conduct the study of White House glass that resulted in this publication.

White House Glassware will serve as a valuable reference for collectors of American glassware. It also documents historic and social activities that have enlivened the White House during the course of nearly two centuries. This book mirrors the teamwork of many talented people. The challenge of photographing the glass to achieve the clarity of detail seen on these pages took the expertise of Corning Museum photographer Nicholas Williams. The critical studio setting could not be duplicated in the White House, and so the glass was shipped to Corning, New York. The results of this effort shine on the following pages.

We are especially grateful to The Corning Museum of Glass, the board of directors of the White House Historical Association, and members of the Special Publications Division of the National Geographic Society for their help in producing a book as remarkable as the glassware itself.

Betty C. Monkman

Associate Curator,
The White House

Contents

Glassware Illustrations

All glassware photography in this book is the work of
Nicholas Williams of The Corning Museum of Glass. All glassware pieces
illustrated, unless otherwise noted with the photograph, are
part of the White House collection.

III. *Abraham Lincoln to Grover Cleveland*
THE LINCOLN SERVICE

Introduction

Much as the crystal ball is said to foretell the future, so the glassware of the Presidents might be said to reflect our past. If only these wineglasses and goblets, decanters and finger bowls could speak to us, what tales they would surely tell.

On these pages I have tried to recapture some of the moments the White House glassware was witness to—as well as to present a survey of the glassware used on the presidential table from Washington's time to the present. In doing so, I have relied on three primary sources: the glassware collection belonging to the White House, the purchase records preserved from each presidential administration, and the inventories taken during many administrations.

The 19th-century records are kept at the National Archives; some have been microfilmed. Certain documents are missing, and, of the existing ones, neither the invoices nor the inventories include much description. Even so, it is possible in some cases to match these up with existing glassware.

The purchases of glassware for presidential use came out of the "furniture fund," money appropriated by Congress at the beginning of each administration. The usual sum varied from around $14,000 to $20,000, but could be supplemented by an additional appropriation if the President so requested. "Furniture," in its 19th-century sense, meant furnishings of all kinds. The furniture fund was expected to cover furniture, decorating expenses such as paint and paper, maintenance and repair, and all sorts of necessities from kitchen equipment to silver knives and forks. Consequently, only a small part of the fund was spent on glassware.

Before 1809 the President usually appointed an agent to purchase the furnishings, although members of the President's personal staff were sometimes authorized to spend the money as well. From 1809 until 1925 the designated purchaser was the

America's first industry, glassmaking employs fire and finesse to create an almost magical liquid product from sand and other ingredients. An 18th-century illustration depicts the craft, brought to the New World in the 1600s by European immigrants. Here, a furnace master stirs the molten ingredients. Then a gatherer dips a blowpipe into the furnace and pulls out a gather, a blob of glass. An assistant smooths the gather on a flat slab. Puffing into the blowpipe, he inflates the gather in a mold selected to give the expanding glass bubble a goblet shape.

official in charge of public buildings in Washington. Invoices were submitted in groups to the Treasury for reimbursement by means of a voucher, and it is these records that include the invoices for glassware. The records of 20th-century purchases are not among the Treasury Department papers at the National Archives, but in the White House itself.

In the early years not all the purchases from the fund were of new items. Sales of secondhand items were common in Washington. European diplomats routinely sold their household contents before moving on to other posts. Perhaps because of this precedent, the appropriations bills authorized the President to sell "decayed" furnishings to raise money for new purchases. Through these sales much presidential glassware and china was dispersed. Breakage of glassware accounts for the loss of a great deal more.

An 1826 federal law mandated that White House furnishings be of American manufacture unless suitable American-made goods were not available. European porcelain dinner services, for example, continued in use at the White House throughout the 19th and into the 20th century because comparable American porcelain was unobtainable. The glassware used with these dinner services on the presidential table, however, was mainly American. In a time when American glass manufacturers were competing against cheaper European imports, this was a matter of pride for the fledgling glass industry.

Since White House glassware was purchased with public funds, it stayed in the House and was not the property of the President and First Lady who had ordered it. Not every first family ordered new glassware, for funds were insufficient to replace the dining equipment every four years. Some Presidents and their wives were less

The dextrous master blower, called a gaffer, sits on a special bench. The blowpipe, tipped with a bubble of glass, rests on the bench's long flat arms. With one hand, he rolls the blowpipe. With his other hand, he deftly plies metal tongs and other simple tools to work the rotating glass. A helper fetches a dab of hot glass. Tooled by the gaffer, it forms the goblet's stem. The gaffer then snips off the excess, as an assistant prepares more glass for the base of the goblet.

PAGES 12–15: REPRODUCED FROM *L'ENCYCLOPEDIE, OU DICTIONNAIRE RAISONNE DES SCIENCES, DES ARTS ET DES METIERS*, DENIS DIDEROT, PARIS, 1762–1772

interested in table furnishings than were others. There are remains of four "state services" of glassware used in the 19th and early 20th centuries as well as the one currently in use. In addition, there are odd pieces of glassware that were used to supplement these services, glassware purchased for presidential family use, and some pieces given to the White House because of their association with a President or his family. Although none of the Presidents had unlimited means when ordering glassware, the elegance of the remaining services is evidence of the high quality of American glass in the 19th century. The services also provide a graphic view of the progression of glassware styles during that period. Most of the state services remained in use for decades, because fashions did not change rapidly. The style currently being used in official entertaining was first purchased in 1961.

In this book "state service" is defined as glassware specially ordered for White House use at state dinners and often engraved with a version of the Great Seal of the United States. There were four to a dozen state dinners a year, but the best glass and porcelain services were probably used at all formal dinners, whether affairs of state or not. The number and formality of White House dinners and receptions varied from one administration to the next. The usual practice in the 19th century was for the President to entertain members of Congress, justices of the Supreme Court, and members of the diplomatic corps each year. As Congress and the diplomatic corps grew in numbers, it became impossible to entertain all the members at dinner once a year, so they were invited to receptions instead. Receptions were also held for other dignitaries and for the public. The New Year's Day reception was usually the largest of these.

President and Mrs. Hayes were the first occupants of the President's House to take real interest in its history and to preserve some of the furnishings. When Hayes left office in 1881, he and his wife returned to Ohio with a selection of pieces from

A second helper attaches a blob of heated glass to the goblet's stem. In the hands of the gaffer, a shaping tool flares the rotating glass into a circular base. Next a pontil, held by one of the helpers, is fused to the center of the base. Now the gaffer can separate goblet and blowpipe in a process called whetting off. With the piece affixed only to the pontil, the gaffer then can begin the finishing touches.

the glass services then in the White House pantry that were too old or too reduced in number for practical use.

Mrs. Benjamin Harrison, a skilled china painter, was the next to take an interest in the glass and chinaware of previous administrations. In 1889 she attempted to form a collection, but she died before her husband left office, and the project was dropped. In 1908 Mrs. Theodore Roosevelt was horrified to find that chipped pieces were sold or given away. She considered this undignified and, at the suggestion of her husband's aide Archibald Butt, decided that chipped glass and china should be crushed and disposed of in the Potomac River to prevent its being sold to the public as souvenirs.

During that administration, at the suggestion of Col. Theodore Bingham, then superintendent of public buildings and grounds, the writer Abby Gunn Baker was retained to inventory the White House tableware collection. She was to link the china and glassware with the proper administrations and to write an article about her findings. As part of her research, Mrs. Baker visited former First Ladies and other members of presidential families, and she rescued a number of pieces from storage, although her identifications were in some cases mistaken. She continued as honorary caretaker of the china and glass collection until her death in 1923. Her work formed the nucleus of the White House tableware collection. Part of that collection has been displayed since 1908 on the ground floor, first in the corridor, then since 1917 in the China Room, which was specially altered for this purpose. The remainder of the collection is either in storage or on loan to the National Museum of American History of the Smithsonian Institution, where it can be enjoyed by more people than have the opportunity to tour the White House.

The furnace side of his face shielded from blistering heat by a hat flap, the gaffer reheats the goblet, twirling it to open up the mouth. Next, he shears away rough edges, perfects the shape, then cracks off the pontil from the goblet. His helper lifts the piece into an annealing oven, where slow cooling tempers the glass. Untempered glass would easily shatter, wasting hours of patient craftsmanship.

The Earliest Glassware

Americans have found fascination in the furnishings of the President's House throughout its history. Each time a First Lady has redecorated a room or chosen new china or glassware for official use, public interest has been stirred. In the 19th century a growing source of pride was the widespread use of American furnishings, important to a new nation just beginning to provide its own manufactured goods. Glassware, in particular, sparked national pride, for American glass manufacturers excelled even while the country was young.

During the first four administrations, however, Americans used English, and sometimes French or Bohemian, glassware. From the end of the Revolution until 1800, only one glasshouse, that of John F. Amelung, in New Bremen, Maryland, was successful in making tableware. After 1808 Benjamin Bakewell's glass factory, in Pittsburgh, Pennsylvania, could have supplied the White House with table glass, but residents of eastern cities were scarcely aware that such a factory existed on the frontier. President James Monroe was first to order a set of American glass for the official residence, but all the pieces of that first American service have disappeared.

FIG. 1. Decanter, one of a pair given to President James Madison in 1816 by Benjamin Bakewell, of Pittsburgh, Pennsylvania. Ht. 8$^{11}/_{16}$". (Gift to the White House collection from the White House Preservation Fund with funds from Mr. and Mrs. Lloyd Rapport and funds in memory of Lila Acheson Wallace, 1986.)

George Washington and John Adams

The first presidential residence was in New York City, where Congress rented the home of Samuel Osgood on Cherry Street for the Washingtons. President Washington moved in during April 1789. Among the articles purchased for use by the Washingtons were "Glass Ware" worth £127 from William Williams and "Glass and Queen's Ware [a kind of pottery]" worth £281 from James Christie, both local merchants.[1] Osgood's niece, writing to a friend, noted that the house was "furnished in the most elegant manner" with "the best of furniture in every room, and the greatest quantity of plate and China that I ever saw before."[2] The glassware bought from Williams and Christie must have been equally elegant.

Washington had insisted on "neat and fashionable" appointments for Mount Vernon, his personal home, and he was no less interested in the furnishings purchased for his official residences. The diplomat Gouverneur Morris, writing from Paris in 1790 after Washington commissioned him to buy tableware, said:

> *I think it of very great importance to fix the taste of our Country properly, and I think your Example will go so very far in that respect. It is therefore my Wish that every Thing about you should be substantially good and majestically plain, made to endure.[3]*

Because Washington wished to establish and maintain the dignity of the new nation and the Presidency, he entertained with stiff formality. On Tuesdays he received callers at levees. These were austere occasions at which neither chairs nor refreshments were offered. Mrs. Washington received visitors from eight to ten on Friday evenings and served lemonade and ice cream.[4] The Washingtons frequently had dinners for 20 to 30 official guests—members of Congress, diplomats, and distinguished visitors. Decanters, wineglasses, and tumblers must have been among the items purchased for these occasions from Williams and Christie.

Washington chose not to accept a salary, but he did regularly submit an expense account. He was careful to distinguish between purchases for Mount Vernon (which he did not submit for reimbursement) and those for official residences. Deciding the Osgood house was too small, Washington moved to a larger one on Broadway. In 1790 the government was moved to Philadelphia, where it would remain for ten years, until the new federal city on the Potomac was ready for occupancy.

The Washingtons began in 1791 a custom that continued until 1932—that of receiving the public on New Year's Day. A visitor has left this description of the first New Year's reception:

> *Just as I passed the President's House, Griffin hailed me and asked whether I would not pay my respects to the President. . . . I was pushed forward by him, . . . made the President the compliments of the season, had a hearty shake by the hand. I was asked to partake of the punch and cake, but declined. I sat down, and we had some chat, but the diplomatic gentry and the foreigners coming in, I embraced the first vacancy to make my bow and wish him good morning.[5]*

The President of the United States, &
requests the Pleasure of Mr & Mrs Bailys
Company to Dine, on Thursday next,
at 4 o'Clock.
Jan 1, 1801
An answer is requested.

First mistress of the White House arrives in 1800. Abigail Adams, helped from the carriage by her husband, John, lived for only a few months in the unfinished mansion. The couple held the first public New Year's Day reception at the White House in 1801, followed by the private dinner noted on the invitation above.

In October 1789 Washington had written to Morris asking him to purchase several table articles in France. On the list were silver wine coolers.[6] He wanted eight double coolers for Madeira and claret to serve with dinner, each to hold two pint decanters. For after-dinner use he wanted four more coolers, each to hold four quart bottles or decanters. He concluded: "One idea . . . I must impress you with and that is . . . to avoid extravagance. For extravagance would not comport with my own inclination, nor with the example which ought to be set."[7] The silver came nearly a year later, and with it came cut-glass decanters, mentioned in another letter.[8]

The account books for May 1792 show the purchase of two glass stands (possibly sweetmeat stands),[9] and in November of that year, the Washingtons purchased glass and china for $34 from James Gallagher, a Philadelphia retailer.[10] There were no more large purchases; instead, replacement items like "12 glass rummers" (a rummer was a large goblet) and "6 wine glasses" appear from time to time.

When Washington left office he rendered an accounting of the furnishings and commented: "Nothing has been said relating to the Table Linnens, Sheeting, China and Glassware which was furnished at the expense of the United States because they have been worn out, broken, stolen and replaced at private expense over and over again."[11] The Washingtons took much of their china and probably some of their glass back to Virginia. Some of the glassware now at Mount Vernon and in the hands of Martha Washington's descendants may have been used in Washington's presidential establishments, but none is sufficiently distinctive to be identified as having been used in the New York and Philadelphia residences.

Incoming President John Adams purchased with government funds a few of the leftover household furnishings of the Washingtons. The remainder were sold the day after the couple left Philadelphia for Mount Vernon. The inventory of furnishings taken in February 1797 separates the objects to be sold from those kept by the

Washingtons. The plated wine coolers purchased by Morris were to be sold; the cut-glass decanters are not mentioned. No glass tableware is on the list to be sold.

John Adams had been authorized "to cause to be sold such parts of the furniture and equipage belonging to his household as may be decayed and out of repair. . . ." Furthermore, Congress authorized "that a sum together with the proceeds of such sale be appropriated for the accommodation of the household of the President."[12] Ever the pessimist, Adams worried about the expense of being President even before his election. He had found it possible to live within the vice presidential salary only when Abigail was in New England and he could omit entertaining. The official residence was sparsely furnished, and John wrote Abigail that "all the glasses [mirrors], ornaments, kitchen furniture, . . . glass and crockery of every sort"[13] would have to be purchased.

The accounts of Adams's furniture purchases are not so detailed as those of Washington's. Adams must have purchased some glassware, for he and Abigail had frequent official dinners for members of the government and for foreign dignitaries. One such dinner was described by a congressman in a letter home to his wife:

We went straight from the House of Representatives to the President's and were introduced by name to the President who shook us by the hand and then he introduced us to Mrs. Adams. . . . We then sat down and the waiter handed round a glass of punch. . . . In a few minutes dinner was announced. . . . There were about twenty-five persons at the table, the utensils were only common blue china plates, glass tumblers and wine glasses and bone handled knives and forks were the best that we had. The table was decorated with glass stands, five in number. On the two extremes were only dishes of common lettuce or salad. Next to these, towards the center at each end was a piece of pastry much resembling a large cake. . . . In the center there was a large cake of the same form but it was incrusted on the sides with a fine white frosted surface, spangled with sugar plums of different colors and on the top were sugar plums of different colors in the shape of cocked hats, shells, radishes, etc.[14]

The letter goes on to describe the soup, more than a dozen meats, two vegetables, and the desserts. The five "glass stands" along the center of the table, holding salad and dessert, were probably footed salvers with flat top surfaces, although the two with "common lettuce" might have been more like compotes. (In some contexts the word "stand" refers to a metal frame holding either a decanter—a bottle stand—or condiments—a cruet stand.) All the glass was almost certainly English, purchased probably from a retail shop in Philadelphia.

In 1800, near the end of his term, John and Abigail Adams moved to Washington to become the first occupants of the President's House. Thomas Claxton, the doorkeeper of the House of Representatives, was assigned to oversee the moving of their furnishings from Philadelphia to the still unfinished residence. There is no detailed list of the furnishings or of what Claxton purchased for the mansion to augment them. Mrs. Adams complained about the lack of amenities, especially the scarcity of lamps. She mentioned that some china was broken or stolen during the move, but she made no mention of glass in her litany of complaints. On January 1, 1801, the Adamses had the first public New Year's Day reception in the new President's House, in the upstairs Oval Drawing Room; by then enough glassware had been unpacked for entertaining.

Before the Adamses moved out a few months later, an inventory was taken, dated February 26, 1801.[15] It listed glass and silver under the heading "Plated Ware." There were "4 Bottle Stands, 1 set of casters complete, 4 Glass baskets." The bottle stands and casters were silver stands holding glass decanters and condiment bottles. Under "Glass Ware" is the laconic entry "A plentiful quantity." It presumably covered wineglasses, tumblers and perhaps serving pieces. No glass articles used during the first two administrations remain in the White House collection.

Thomas Jefferson

Thomas Jefferson next moved into the partially furnished mansion. According to the inventory of 1801, he had plenty of glassware for his first term in office. He gave up the formal levees held by Washington and Adams, and he did not care for large, formal dinner parties. Jefferson had been a widower for many years; his daughters and Dolley Madison, the wife of his secretary of state, acted as hostesses for him when necessary.

A contemporary description of Jefferson's dinners indicates that he usually invited 12 to 14 guests. He preferred that they help themselves, so that servants would not need to be present. Margaret Bayard Smith, wife of the editor of the *National Intelligencer* newspaper, dined with Jefferson many times; she described his oval or circular table arrangement, which promoted easy conversation, and praised his meals:

> *The whole of Mr. Jefferson's domestic establishment at the Presidents House exhibited good taste and good judgement. . . . The excellence and superior skill of his French cook was acknowledged by all who frequented his table, for never before had such dinners been given in the President's House, nor such a variety of the finest and most costly wines. In his entertainments, republican simplicity was united to Epicurean delicacy while the absence of splendour ornament and profusion was more than compensated by the neatness, order and elegant sufficiency that pervaded the whole establishment.[16]*

Mrs. Smith also noted that

> *One great reform in dining parties was made by Mr. Jefferson; instead of remaining for hours at table after the ladies had withdrawn, at his parties, the gentlemen after taking two or three glasses of wine, left the table and took their coffee in the drawing room, which custom not only preserved temperance, but promoted the most refined social enjoyment.[17]*

Thomas Claxton handled the purchases from the furniture fund for Jefferson during both his terms, but the only glass purchases that can be traced were made late in the second term. Glass was combined with crockery and not itemized in most of the accounts. Only one account, covering October 13, 1808, to January 1, 1809, has the vouchers still attached. It lists "Silver Ware, China and Glass Ware and the repairing of the clock."[18] The china and glass were purchased from Thompson & Moxley, local merchants, for $111.80 on October 4, 1808, and included 6 sweetmeat glasses and "3 doz. Best cut tumblers." The sweetmeat glasses were conical, footed glasses used for desserts like ice creams, puddings, jellies, and syllabubs.

Obviously, much more glass was purchased. Jefferson's inventory of February 19, 1809, lists the following in the large dining room:

Glass

30 Decanters	*13 Oval Crystals for Sweet Meats*
9 Water bottles	*27 [Oval Crystals] Small*
4 [Water bottles] small	*48 Wine Glasses*
72 Tumblers	*20 liqueur Glasses*
75 Jelly Glasses	*2 Water Pitchers*
72 Wine Glasses	

and in the small dining room:

2 Sallad dishes with glasses	*3 Cans*
16 Goblets	*10 Barrel tumblers*[19]

Some may have been among the "plentiful quantity" left by the Adamses.

Jefferson, known for the quantity and quality of the wines he served, spent more than $10,000—a prodigious sum—on wine in the eight years of his Presidency. His purchases included Madeira, claret, sauterne, burgundy, and champagne—from France, Spain, Portugal, Italy, Germany, and Hungary.[20] From the mention of tumblers in the list of glassware above, it appears that Jefferson served whiskey as well.

The term "jelly glass" in the inventory was another name for "sweetmeat glass," used for desserts. Jefferson's small gatherings would have required service for no more than two dozen. At large receptions jelly glasses would have been used for serving sweets like ice creams and jellies. Since Jefferson held few large receptions, the jelly glasses may have been left over from Abigail Adams's entertaining.

James Madison

James and Dolley Madison entertained much more frequently and even more lavishly than did Jefferson. Dolley understood the value of entertaining in promoting her husband's policies.

With the architect Benjamin Latrobe as her purchasing agent, Mrs. Madison set to work to make the President's House a suitable setting for her parties. The couple already owned a quantity of French glassware purchased from James and Elizabeth Monroe in 1803.[21] Among this lot was a pair of silver and cut-glass cruet stands (fig. 2) bought by the Monroes in France, probably while he was minister to France in the 1790s. Though personal possessions of the Madisons from their Virginia house, Montpelier, the stands have been given to the White House.

Dolley's dinner parties were twice as large as Jefferson's. Dolley also entertained on Wednesday evenings at a reception called a "drawing room" that seems to have been similar to the Washingtons' evening receptions. Such occasions would have required wineglasses and tumblers for whiskey punch and wine. Lord Francis Jeffrey, who called on the Madisons in 1813, mentioned the libations served:

We were shown across a very large handsome hall, but quite unfurnished, to a little parlour. . . . The President himself entered [and] . . . pointed out to us a most base and paltry glass ship about a foot long, such a thing as one sets on the mantle piece of our ale houses in England which was placed on a stand. . . . Wine and liqueurs were handed round with some stale cake, and we retired with three long and laborious bows from the archenemy.[22]

Lord Jeffrey was not disposed to charity toward the Madisons—his country was then at war with the United States. At the Wednesday evening drawing room, Jeffrey saw 50 to 60 people, mostly Army and Navy officers and bureaucrats, whom he described as respectable but dull. "They had again cake," he writes, "and salvers with glasses of wine and little cups of what I took for lemonade but found to my infinite horror was strong punch." Later he dined at the White House, at

> *a long table with a tarnished flat plateau [a large centerpiece] in the cen-*
> *tre . . . no plate and no china—ordinary blue English ware, a very few little*
> *bottles with white wine, and as few of claret in its native French bottles, all*
> *very middling. . . . After dinner three cracked decanters . . . with a little*
> *thing like a vinegar cruet to supply the want of the fourth, and in this style the*
> *wine was decanted to thirty people.*[23]

Jefferson had received and spent a total of $29,000 from the furniture fund for his two terms; Madison had $20,000 to spend during the first six years of his Presidency. More than a thousand dollars of that sum was spent on tableware, some of it glass. In December 1810 and January 1811 John Thompson sold the White House 24 tumblers, a dozen wineglasses, and 18 lemonade cans (mugs).[24] In October 1811 Charles Moxley, no longer in partnership with Thompson as he had been when they sold glass to Jefferson, supplied "2 doz cut wine glasses, 1 pare cut Decanters, 1 doz cut tumblers," and on November 4, another two dozen wineglasses.[25]

The next Moxley invoice lists two dozen "best cut tumblers" and a pair of "best cut decanters."[26] There is no indication in any of the invoices that the tumblers and wineglasses were intended to match or form a set or that the decanters matched any of the glasses. It seems plain that the Madisons were purchasing from stock.

In 1812 Michael Kromenacker, a local merchant, sold the White House three dozen cut wineglasses and two dozen ice cream glasses.[27] The following October John Thompson supplied "4 water carrofts" and, in November, two dozen tumblers, three dozen wineglasses, and two pitchers.[28] In 1813 purchasing agent Lewis Deblois bought 63 tumblers, 30 wineglasses, six glass salts, and 11 claret glasses at a public sale.[29] These probably were secondhand. Later that year Deblois made a large purchase of china and glass from Woodward and Cooke, Georgetown retailers, which included "3 Doz Cut and E. [engraved] wine" and "1 Doz. Tumblers Best English Glass."[30] In 1814 Deblois bought "20 elegant Beer glasses" at auction.[31]

These purchases totaled 143 tumblers, 247 wineglasses and goblets, eight decanters and carafes, and two pitchers, probably decorated by cutting and/or engraving. Much of this glassware was likely to have been English—easily available as well as fashionable. Some may have been French and Bohemian.

On August 24, 1814, all that remained of this glass was destroyed when the British burned the White House toward the end of the War of 1812. We know from Mrs. Madison's own account that—although she saved some silver and two boxes of state papers—the other furnishings, including many personal items, were lost. One contemporary account indicates that the dining room was prepared for the midday meal when Dolley fled, with plates warming and wine in the cut-glass decanters. The British officers were said to have served themselves before they set the fire.[32]

Following the fire the White House was left a roofless shell. The Madisons were forced to live in rented quarters at Octagon House, the mansion of Col. John Tayloe, until March 1815. They then moved to the Seven Buildings, a group of joined houses, until the end of Madison's term.

The pace of the Madisons' entertaining did not slacken despite their lack of an official residence. They purchased more glass, some of it secondhand because it was more easily available. From a brother-in-law, Richard Cutts, the Madisons bought two dozen water goblets and champagnes, five dozen tumblers, four dozen wineglasses, and two dozen jelly glasses, all described as "double flint cut glass."[33] From a Mrs. Buchanan, they bought a pair of cut-glass pitchers, a pair of cut-glass decanters, and a pair of cut water carafes.[34] Local merchants also sold the Madisons glassware: Tumblers and wineglasses came from Mrs. Lear[35] and from A. L. Joncherez, who supplied seven dozen wineglasses, two pairs of decanters, and two dozen tumblers in 1816.[36] Charles A. Burnett, a local silversmith, supplied two dozen each of tumblers and wineglasses and a dozen champagne glasses in 1817.[37] The final purchase included six glass dishes bought from Samuel McKenney that year.[38]

As a gift, the Madisons received a pair of beautifully cut decanters (figs. 1, 3) from Bakewell, Page and Bakewell, glass manufacturers of Pittsburgh. The firm had been started in 1808 by Benjamin Bakewell, who saw that colonists on the western frontier needed glass. Although other factories were producing bottles and window glass, Bakewell's glasshouse was the first to make fine lead-glass tableware profitably. The decanters were sent to Madison on February 19, 1816, with this letter:

> *Sir, convinced that you who have devoted so large a portion of your life to the promotion of the welfare of Independance of our Country, will not look with indifference upon the progress she is making in the Arts and Manufactures, we take the liberty of sending you a pair of decanters made and cut at our manufactory and of which we request the favor of your acceptance.*
>
> *When it is recollected that all the materials for making glassware are found abundantly in our own soil and how large this article contributes to the comforts, conveniences and elegancies of life, we flatter ourselves you will derive as much pleasure from receiving this specimen as we in furnishing it.*[39]

A personal gift to the Madisons, the decanters were taken home to Montpelier in 1817. Years later, in an 1846 list in the handwriting of Payne Todd, Dolley's son, "2 decanters, Pittsburgh" appears. Sometime in the next 20 years, the decanters were given or sold to a relative, because one of them was offered to the Massachusetts Historical Society in 1867; it was described as "A very handsome cut glass Decanter which was presented to Mr. Madison by the manufactory at Pittsburgh, Pa., Engraved with armorials of the U. S. and the letter M."[40] Massachusetts Historical Society records do not name the person who offered the decanter for sale, along with a portrait of James Madison by Charles Willson Peale and other Madison relics. In the same year the Madison portrait, the only one painted by Peale, was sold to the Long Island Historical Society by a Mrs. Helen Madison. Perhaps a relative of the President, she was thus likely to have been the owner of the decanters.[41]

By the turn of the century the pair of decanters had come into the possession of the Douglas Robinson family, descendants of President James Monroe's nephew, and were thought to be Monroe souvenirs. During one of several fires at the Robinson house, the decanters lost their stoppers, and one was badly broken, then subsequently repaired. In 1984 and 1985 the decanters were sold by the Robinsons.[42] One went to the White House and the other to a private collector.

They are stunning examples of the diamond-cut style then popular and much more elaborate than the pieces usually attributed to Bakewell. Their engraving of

the eagle and shield, taken from the Great Seal of the United States, is the earliest known use of this design as a symbol of the Presidency. Some variation of it was subsequently to be used on White House glass and china throughout the 19th century and into the 20th. The eagle was a popular symbol of the United States from the Revolutionary period until the mid-19th century, and it may be found inlaid in furniture, engraved on glass and silver, painted on porcelain, and ornamenting a host of other decorative furnishings.

James Monroe

When James Monroe took office in 1817 the White House had not been sufficiently restored for his family to move in. In March of that year Congress appropriated $20,000 for the furniture fund. Monroe asked a friend, William Lee, to oversee the furnishing of the house, although Samuel Lane was responsible for disbursing the money. Lee immediately visited the former residence of the Madisons to see if anything there was usable in the White House. His conclusion: "There was no recourse in the remnants of glass, earthenware, china, linen, etc. of which scarcely an article would serve indeed we may say there remained none of these articles fit for use."[43] With the large amount of glassware purchased the previous year for the Madisons, this is surprising, but it shows the toll social life took on the tableware.

Monroe decided to sell some of his own imported French furnishings for use in the mansion and made arrangements to have them valued on March 15, 1817.[44] Monroe's glassware consisted of two pairs of decanters, 18 claret glasses, 49 wineglasses, six tumblers, four pairs of salt dishes, and a "Glass Plateau, Silver Plated Rim" that, at $200, was the most valuable glass item on the list. These items thus went to the White House with the Monroes and remained there.

Most of Monroe's appropriation was spent on furniture, silver, porcelain, and other articles ordered from France. The shipment arrived in November 1817.

Flames set by British troops gut the White House during the War of 1812. The enemy struck on the evening of August 24, 1814. According to an account of the time, Dolley Madison had ordered the dining room set for the midday meal while her husband witnessed the nearby Battle of Bladensburg. Plates were warming and wine waiting in cut-glass decanters. The alarm cry of a battlefield messenger sent her fleeing to safety, with little time to salvage possessions. The fire destroyed nearly all the furnishings, including the imported glassware.

PAINTING BY LESLIE SAALBURG,
COURTESY MAC G. MORRIS

FIG. 2. French silver cruet set, one of a pair purchased by James Monroe in France and sold by him in 1803 to James and Dolley Madison. Silver by Roch-Louis Dany, France, 1789; glass bottles are replacements purchased in 1931. Ht. 12 7/8". (Bequest, in 1931, of James Clark McGuire, grandson of James C. McGuire, who had acquired them in partial payment of a debt owed by Payne Todd, Dolley Madison's son.)

Because the White House had to be completely refurnished, the money soon ran out, and a second sum of $30,000 was appropriated.

Meanwhile, in September 1817, the President had visited Pittsburgh, where he toured Benjamin Bakewell's glasshouse. Bakewell's establishment was then nine years old. As the largest of several glass factories in the city, it was a magnet for visitors. Many who toured the factory later published accounts of it and of the English-style cut glass made there. Henry B. Fearon, an Englishman who visited Bakewell's glasshouse that year, wrote:

> *I was astonished to witness such perfection on this side of the Atlantic and especially in that part of America which a New Yorker supposes to be at the farther end of the world. At Messrs. Page and Bakewell's glass warehouse I*

saw chandeliers and numerous articles in cut glass of a very splendid description; among the latter was a pair of decanters, cut from a London pattern. . . .[45]

The proprietor, one of the community's leading citizens, presented Monroe with a pair of cut-glass decanters as he had President Madison. No record has been found that describes the pair, however. During the visit, or shortly thereafter, Monroe ordered from Bakewell a set of glassware for the White House; full documentation for this still exists, although no pieces of the glass are known to have survived.

Monroe's orders of expensive furnishings from France had caused some controversy. Certain citizens felt that nationalism and support of local manufacturers were more important than the dictates of fashion. A New England newspaper ran the following article in November, after the French shipment had arrived:

It is now stated, that the articles of furniture, imported from France, for the President's house, were such only as could not be procured in this country. The President himself directed, that his cut glass should be purchased at Pittsburgh (Penn) and exertions were made to complete the orders, as far as practicable, in the City of Washington.[46]

The set of glassware was finished in November 1818, and the *Pittsburgh Gazette* printed a full description of it on November 10:

During a visit a few evenings ago to the manufactory of Messrs. Bakewells' and Page, we were much gratified by a sight of the splendid equipage of glass, intended for Mr. Munroe's sideboard. It consists of a full set of Decanters, Wine Glasses and Tumblers of various sizes and different models, exhibiting a brilliant specimen of double flint, engraved and cut by Jardelle. This able artist has displayed his best manner, and the arms of the United States on each piece have a fine effect. The glass itself must either have been selected with great care, or the spirited proprietors must have made considerable progress in their art, for we have seldom seen any samples so perfectly pellucid and free from tinct. Upon the whole we think the present service equal, if not superior to the elegant Decanters presented to the President when he passed through Pittsburgh last year.

It affords us a most sensible gratification that the patriotic liberality of Mr. Munroe will give us the opportunity of being known to the world, as proficients in some of the most delicate branches of manufactures; as regards cloth, iron ware, and the common production of glass, we consider our reputation as long established; we may now calculate upon increasing this reputation by the addition of the branch of chrystall glass, since such a man as James Munroe looks to Pittsburgh for this article. We cannot forbear congratulating Messrs. Bakewell & Page on this occasion; their meritorious struggles are at length crowned with partial success; may the policy to be adopted by our government be such as, at no very distant day, to insure them that reward, which their urbanity, enterprise and industry merit, and may the "glass that sparkles" on the President's "board" operate as a talisman on our representatives, to stimulate them to unremitting exertions in favor of manufactures.[47]

FIG. 3. *Engraved insignia on the decanter in figure 1. Derived from the Great Seal of the United States (top), the design bears the initial of James Madison, the "Father of the Constitution." The bald eagle, symbol of authority, represents the government; a sheaf of arrows, the national defense; an olive branch, peace.*

The invoice, which is still in the National Archives,[48] lists two shipments, one dated November 14, 1818, of

12 doz cut Tumblers at	*$15 per doz*
8 [doz cut] Wines	*$12*
4 [doz cut] clarets	*$13 ¹/₂*
6 pr. Cut qt. decanters	*$30*

With U. S. arms engraved on each.

This was obviously the glass described in the preceding newspaper article. On the same page is a second shipment, dated February 16, 1819, of

6 pr. water decanters	*$40 per pair*
2 pr. 13" oval dishes	*$40 [per pair]*
6 pr 9" [oval dishes]	*$25 [per pair]*
6 pr. salts	*$ 8 [per pair]*

No mention of the U. S. arms appears under the second list; but since the prices are similar, the second group was probably also engraved. The bill for $1,032, which included packing and shipping charges, was not paid until December 13, 1821, more than two years after the glass was received.

Because none of the Monroe glass set remains, it is impossible to be certain of the style in which it was cut, but it seems likely that the glass was decorated in the strawberry-diamond motif then fashionable in England and in the United States. That motif had fields of crosshatched diamonds or small diamonds within large ones. Surviving Bakewell glasses like the large urn in the Yale Art Gallery (similar to a pair made for the Marquis de Lafayette in 1824) and the Madison decanters made in 1816 are heavily cut in this style. The cutting was probably done by Bakewell's regular staff, and the U. S. arms were engraved by Alexander Jardel, a French glass engraver who had recently moved to Pittsburgh and opened a shop.[49] The engraved arms may have been copied from the French porcelain dessert service that had arrived in 1817, or from the engraving on Madison's decanters, which resembled more closely the Great Seal of the United States.

In December 1819 the Monroes received a splendid gift from the New England Glass Company, a concern started the year before in Cambridge, Massachusetts. Perhaps because of the publicity given to the President's set of Pittsburgh glassware, the company presented a gift of its own, a large covered vase of richly cut glass, valued at $500. It had been cut by John Fisher and John Gilliland (each later had his own glasshouse in New York). The *Niles Weekly Register*, a Baltimore paper that promoted American manufactures, reported:

> *It is an Urn, and consists of three pieces, the base, the bowl and the cover, weighing 45 pounds, intended for the central ornament of a table. The cutting on the foot is in arched scollops, flutings and deep splits with prismatic rings and splits beneath the bowl round the bottom, in the language of the manufactory, has raised diamonds and deep sunk rings; and on the body . . . deeper strawberry diamonds, rings and arched scollops; the cover has a cheverel cut from the solid glass, edge arched scollops, prismatic rings with splits beneath; rows of strawberry diamonds and . . . raised diamonds.[50]*

This wonderful specimen of American glass has disappeared, along with the pair of decanters monogrammed *A* that the New England Glass Company presented at the same time to John Quincy Adams, then Secretary of State.[51]

The Monroes entertained well. The New Year's reception in 1821, after James Monroe had been reelected, was typical. Said a letter writer from Virginia:

> *Mr. Monroe was standing near the door, and, as we were introduced, we had the honor of shaking hands with him and passing the usual congratulations of the season. . . . Mrs. Monroe's manner is very gracious, and she is a regal-looking lady. . . . All the lower rooms were opened and they were warmed by great fires of hickory wood, and with the handsome brass andirons and fenders quite reminded me of our grand old wood fires in Virginia. Wine was handed about in wine-glasses on large silver salvers, by colored waiters dressed in dark livery, gilt buttons, etc.*[52]

Monroe's last glassware was bought in January 1822 from a Philadelphia merchant. Included were six dozen fluted tumblers, six dozen wineglasses, two dozen champagne glasses, and two pairs of quart decanters.[53] In all $132 was spent for this glass; and since the price per dozen was about half that of the Bakewell glass, it was probably neither cut nor engraved. When the Monroes left the White House they took with them the New England Glass Company urn and the Bakewell decanters, which had been personal gifts. Both have disappeared.

In 1822 Samuel Lane, Monroe's purchasing agent, died unexpectedly, leaving his accounts in such a state of confusion that $20,000 of government money could not be accounted for. Eventually, to make certain that his own name and reputation were not sullied, the President presented a full accounting of the furniture fund money to a committee of the House of Representatives.[54] The event made a deep impression on John Quincy Adams, who resolved that while in the White House he would manage his furniture fund himself.

The inventory of March 25, 1825, at the beginning of John Quincy Adams's administration, shows 207 pieces of glassware, about two-thirds of the 1818–19 Bakewell shipments.[55] The totals were

12 Large elegant cut water decanters
12 [Large elegant cut] wine [decanters] ⎫
4 Plain [decanters] ⎬ *5 stoppers deficient*
3 Large Preserve dishes ⎭
9 Second size [dishes]
12 Salt cellers
4 [Salt cellars]
23 Cut glass tumblers
39 Champaigne glasses
89 Wine glasses

The number of serving pieces in the inventory was nearly the same as that in the original Bakewell order, but only 23 tumblers remained of the 144 in the original order. The stemware suffered less, for only seven wineglasses and nine claret or champagne glasses were missing. Either the cheaper stemware ordered later was missing from the inventory (although the decanters bought at the same time were the third item), or the plainer wineglasses were included with the engraved ones in the totals.

29

John Quincy Adams

FIG. 4. Ale glass and wineglass owned by President John Quincy Adams and probably by his parents, President and Mrs. John Adams. England, 1765–80. Ht. of taller 7³/₄″. (Gift to the White House collection in 1915 from Mrs. Bowman H. McCalla, who acquired them from Mrs. Archibald Campbell. She had received them from Elizabeth and Hull Adams, niece and nephew of John Quincy Adams.)

The John Quincy Adamses had little need of more glassware, and only one purchase is recorded. In April 1825 Mrs. Adams purchased from A. B. Waller two dozen knob tumblers, three dozen flint tumblers, and two dozen cut wineglasses.[56] The Adamses entertained elegantly, holding formal receptions twice a month. Refreshments for an evening—usually cake, coffee, ice cream, and hot and cold drinks that included sangaree and negus—are said to have cost the President about $50. Here is one visitor's tepid description of a levee:

> *Commencing at seven in the evening, it continued to nearly eleven, the three front rooms were brilliantly lighted with lustres, and the company entered at the eastern gate passing through the large hall where hats, greatcoats and servants were deposited. . . . There was nothing but talking, squeezing, promenading, bowing, drinking coffee and sipping liqueurs.[57]*

The President's opinion of the receptions, confided to his diary, was more to the point: "This evening was the sixth drawing room. Very much crowded; sixteen Senators, perhaps sixty members of the House of Representatives, and multitudes of strangers. . . . These parties are becoming more and more insupportable."[58]

The White House collection has two English wineglasses, which descended in the Adams family (fig. 4). They are believed to have been used by John Quincy Adams and his wife. However, the glasses probably date from the third quarter of the 18th century and would have been quite old-fashioned during the term of the first John Adams as well as his son's. These may be glasses that the second President Adams inherited from his parents and continued to use for family meals, though they were too dated for use in official entertaining.

John Quincy Adams, Jr., in charge of his father's furniture fund, made an accounting to Congress in February 1826. He stressed the strict economy that governed the purchases: "Scarcely an Article has been purchased which was not indispensably necessary; everything has been procured when possible in this City or District, in order to avoid the expenses of transportation. . . ."[59]

Economy notwithstanding, the Adamses spent most of their appropriation in the first year and asked for more. The members of Congress were not entirely happy about this, and when the bill was passed, after some bitter arguments, another bill was enacted specifying that "all furniture purchased for the use of the President's House shall be as far as practicable of American or domestic manufacture."[60]

This act had far-reaching consequences for American glass manufacturers. Although Presidents continued to buy imported chinaware and other furnishings, their glassware appears to have been "of domestic manufacture."

The Jackson and Pierce Services

The oldest remaining glass service at the White House was ordered by Andrew Jackson in 1829 from Bakewell, Page and Bakewell, in Pittsburgh. This service, here called the Jackson-pattern service, was later supplemented by Jackson, then by his successor, Martin Van Buren, and by several other Presidents. It was in use until Franklin Pierce bought a new service—possibly with a new pattern—in 1853.

The Jackson service was cut in flat panels, a style that was rapidly becoming the most fashionable. Panel-cutting was soon to surpass in popularity strawberry-diamond cutting, the Anglo-Irish style prevailing since the end of the 18th century. Both styles were cut during the late 1820s and the 1830s, but after 1840 strawberry-diamond cutting almost disappeared for about 30 years. The few surviving glass-house catalogs from the period—all English—show mainly panel-cut pieces.

Because replacements for and additions to the Jackson-pattern service were ordered over a period of more than 20 years, the pieces do not always match in pattern and in shape. Each piece, however, is engraved with grapevines and grapes as well as a coat of arms (figs. 5, 6) based on the Great Seal of the United States (page 27). The Great Seal, designed in 1782, has always been a popular motif in the decorative arts. On the glassware insignia an eagle perches on a shield of stars and stripes. A banner below contains the motto *E Pluribus Unum.* On the Great Seal the eagle grasps an olive branch in its right talon and a bundle of arrows in its left. A curious departure from tradition on the Jackson glassware is that, instead of the olive branch, there is a palm frond near the eagle's right talon. A laurel branch on the eagle's left replaces the arrows. Both the palm and the laurel are symbols of victory.

FIG. 5. Compote or center dish from the service originally ordered by President Andrew Jackson from Bakewell, Page and Bakewell in 1829. Ht. 11 1/8".

Andrew Jackson

Unprecedented crowds flocked to Washington to see Andrew Jackson, hero of the Battle of New Orleans, take the oath of office on March 4, 1829. The defeated John Quincy Adams indicated in his diary that the customary end-of-term White House inventory was planned. Adams, however, did not want the inventory to be done before all his belongings had been removed.[61] It was doubtless deferred until after Jackson's inauguration.

*Scrappy frontiersman
Andrew Jackson
championed the common
people. A major general in
the War of 1812, Jackson
became a national
hero when he defeated the
British at New Orleans.
During his Presidency
from 1829 to 1837 "Old
Hickory" purchased
a presidential glassware
service in a new pattern,
the oldest one remaining
at the White House.*

DETAIL OF PORTRAIT BY RALPH E. W. EARL
WHITE HOUSE COLLECTION

Following the inaugural ceremony, thousands of people went to the White House for a public reception. Most wanted to glimpse the new President and perhaps to shake his hand, but the crowd was so huge that few could get near him. Eventually Jackson returned to his hotel to escape the mobs of well-wishers. Meanwhile, the crowd fought over the refreshments. Said one witness:

> *Orange punch by barrels full was made but as the waiters opened the door to bring it out, a rush would be made, the glasses broken, the pails of liquor upset and the most painful confusion prevailed. To such a degree was this carried, that wine and ice-cream could not be brought out to the ladies. . . .*[62]

Another writer, visiting later in the day, described "a rabble, a mob of boys, negroes, women, children, scrambling, fighting, romping."[63] She thought that several thousand dollars' worth of cut glass and china had been broken by the crowds. Still another observer reported, "The throng in the rooms was immense, and the tubs of refreshments were necessarily placed outside for the crowd, in order to prevent them from employing very summary methods of getting at them."[64]

Estimates of the size of the crowd varied from 10,000 to 30,000. There seems to be no doubt that the mob was extremely destructive. Under these circumstances, the postponed inventory may never have taken place. A detailed account of the damages would certainly have been embarrassing to the new President. No evidence exists to indicate that the listing was actually done, and no mention of it has yet been found in the National Archives.

Jackson was granted the usual sum of $14,000 for furnishings—though if the damage reports are correct, he must have needed a good bit more. In March 1831 he was voted an additional $5,000, and at the end of the first term, another $20,000.[65] With this money, Jackson finished the East Room—the large reception room where Abigail Adams had hung laundry. He also bought a set of French porcelain and a new service of cut glassware. The glassware, in the first new White House pattern since the Monroes', was ordered from Bakewell, Page and Bakewell, the firm that had supplied Monroe. The 435 pieces cost $1,451.75, with packing and shipping.[66] When Monroe had ordered his set, there was probably not another factory in the country that could have produced it. But by 1829 Bakewell had several competitors on the East Coast as well as in Pittsburgh and in Wheeling, West Virginia.

Because Jackson was a Westerner and familiar with Bakewell's glass, it is not surprising that he ordered his cut glass from Pittsburgh rather than from an eastern firm. The Bakewell firm had presented Mrs. Jackson with a pair of cut celery vases in 1825.[67] Celery vases or glasses—often known simply as "celeries"—were used for serving leafy celery stalks. Celery was then a hothouse vegetable, not readily available, and was given a place of prominence on the table. The Bakewell company had also given Jackson a cut tumbler with his own ceramic portrait in the base in 1828.[68] The company had made a number of such tumblers, with portraits of Lafayette, DeWitt Clinton, Jackson, Washington, and other notables, beginning in 1824 when Lafayette made his triumphal tour of the United States.

There is almost no description of the White House glassware on the Bakewell invoice; it is simply characterized as "richest cut." The following pieces were included (prices are per dozen or per pair):

12 doz richest cut tumblers	*@ $20.00*
6 pr. cut decanters to match	*@ $28.00*

WHITE HOUSE COLLECTION

Thousands storm the White House for a public reception during Jackson's term. At his 1829 inaugural reception, the crowd was so huge that Jackson retreated to a hotel, leaving the mob to fight over the White House refreshments. A witness was dismayed to see "men, with boots heavy with mud, standing on the damask satin-covered chairs." The celebrators shattered perhaps thousands of dollars' worth of cut glass and china.

5 doz. [cut] wines to [match]	@ $18.00
1 Elegant cut Center Bowl & Stand	@ $40.00
2 [Elegant] smaller [Bowl & Stand]	@ $30.00
6 cut Floating Islan[d] dishes	@ $15.00
7 doz. cut Wines to match	@ $18.00
6 doz. [cut] Clarets	@ $20.00
6 pr. Cut pint decanters	@ $20.00
3 pr [Cut] Celeries to match	@ $20.00
6 pr. Cut Pitchers to match	@ $30.00
6 pr. Salts and Stands	@ $10.00
2 pr. 11 Inch Cut dishes to match	@ $20.00
2 pr 9 [Inch Cut dishes to match]	@ $15.00
2 pr 7 [Inch Cut dishes to match]	@ $12.00

The order must have been placed soon after the reception of March 4, because the glassware was ready by July 25, 1829, when a Pittsburgh newspaper said:

That order is nearly completed. We had last week an opportunity of witnessing this splendid exhibit of American skill and ingenuity. It consists of large and splendid bowls with and without stand, celery glasses, pitchers, quart and pint decanters, tumblers, wine and champagne glasses, salts, etc., etc., the whole tastefully decorated in the very best style of workmanship. The glass is pellucid as crystal and beautiful cuttings give brilliancy of effect not easily described. We think the specimen of American workmanship will vie with the best production of French and English articles.[69]

The following month the *Connecticut Courant* reported:

A Box containing a complete set of CUT GLASS *manufactured at Pittsburgh, Pennsylvania, of exquisitely fine workmanship which surpasses anything of*

> *the kind we have ever seen in this country and seldom, if ever, surpassed in Europe; was taken on board the Steamer Columbia, Capt. Mitchell, on Saturday for Washington, as a present for President Jackson.*[70]

Whether this represents more glass—a present for Jackson like the decanters given to Madison and Monroe in previous years—or whether it is simply a garbled account of the White House order is unclear. Jackson did order from Bakewell a set of wines and tumblers for himself. Some of that glassware is now at the Hermitage, his home near Nashville, Tennessee. That order, however, was placed in 1832.[71]

Jackson's dinners were informal, but lavish, if we may believe a young man named Robert Caldwell, who dined with the President in 1834:

> *3 o'clock, the dining hour, found me introduced into the anti-chamber . . . the Prest. entered and there we sat some 15 minutes or so chatting, . . . entered another very finely furnished room which . . . contained two tables richly laden with fine plate and dishes and tall splendid lamps burning on either table—around one table were the chairs which showed that that was the one at which we were to sit . . . nicely folded Knapkin on each plate, with a slice of good light bread in the middle of it. Well, all being seated, the Gen. asked a blessing then the servants about the table, I believe one to every man commenced. . . . Well, the beef being through with away goes your plate and a clean one comes. . . . Fish being through, a new plate and then some other dish. Then a new plate and the pies—then the dessert—then and in the meantime the wines—sherry, madeira, and champagne which are filled into the glasses by the Butler, and then with a significant nod of the head drink [to] one another's health . . . we rise from the table and retire again to the chamber whence we had come, where being seated and in conversation, in comes a servant with a dish of coffee for each of us.*[72]

The dinner lasted four hours, with several choices offered during each course. Jackson, like Jefferson, wished to be considered a plain man of the people, but he also enjoyed living well.

Several years later more glass and china were needed. The Philadelphia firm of Lewis Veron was called in to survey the White House furnishings and make suggestions. An undated "Estimate" attached to the Jackson accounts says:

> *Upon the examination of the China I find it is very broken up and what does remain is very defaced. . . . The glass is in the same situation and must be supplied with a new sett. The many articles remaining from the last set such as dishes, some large size decanters 5 which are not used . . . could be sold with advantage for the public. . . .*[73]

New services of dinner and dessert china for 50 people were estimated by Veron to cost $2,500; a new glass service was estimated at $800. This is substantially less than had been spent at Bakewell's, but the service was to be smaller. The 1829 service from Bakewell had included wineglasses for five to seven dozen people.

A public sale was held in December 1833, and "various pieces of china and glass" were sold, including two center dishes, six glass bowls on feet, four oblong dishes in three sizes, four celeries, 16 saltcellars and stands, 12 decanters, two liquor bottles, 12 water bottles, and other items, which might have been either china or glass.[74] This listing may represent the remains of Monroe's service, which had included oval dishes; the serving pieces from that set would likely have survived Jackson's inaugural reception. Breakage was always worst among tumblers and wineglasses; serving pieces tended to last through several administrations. It seems unlikely that many of Jackson's new serving pieces would have been chipped and offered for sale. Water bottles were included in the 1818 order, and they appear on the 1825 inventory. The 1829 order does not include water bottles, so the ones sold in 1833 must have been purchased in 1818.

The Veron firm sold to President Jackson in December 1833 a "Sett of Table Glass," including

12 doz Champagne glasses	@ $ 8.50 a doz.
12 doz Clarets	@ $ 7.50 [a doz.]
12 doz. Wines	@ $ 6.50 a doz.
6 doz. [Wines] straight stem	@ $ 6.50 [a doz.]
12 doz. Tumblers	@ $ 8.00 [a doz.]
6 doz. Goblets	@ $11.00 [a doz.]
2½ doz. cordials	@ $ 6.00 [a doz.]
9 pr. quart decanters	@ $18.00 a pair
6 do. claret [decanters] with handles	@ $22.00 [a pair]
4 doz. water bottles	@ $36 a doz.[75]

FIG. 6. *The engraved insignia on the compote in figure 5. Like the motifs on earlier insignia, the eagle and shield on the Jackson pattern derive from the Great Seal. Engravers often modified elements of the seal, however. Jackson's emblem choice includes palm frond instead of olive branch, and laurel branch instead of arrows.*

Lewis Veron's glass suppliers have not been identified. A glasshouse in Philadelphia, the Union Glass Company, might have supplied the set, or Veron might have ordered it from Pittsburgh, New York, or New England. The new service is unlikely to have been imported, since Congress had recently passed the law mandating American furnishings for the White House. Jackson himself would have scorned the purchase of imported glass; he was a firm supporter of American manufacturers.

The order totaled $924 for 828 pieces—considerably less per item than the Bakewell order. The price difference between the two might tempt one to conclude that the glass must have been totally different in decoration, but a study of the shapes ordered during Jackson's administration and several that followed suggests otherwise. Furthermore, since few new serving pieces were ordered, the White House must have expected to use the old ones. The new glassware, therefore, was probably in the same pattern as the Bakewell order, though it may not have matched it exactly. Until 1853 few serving pieces except decanters and water bottles were re-ordered, so it seems that Jackson's original pattern from Bakewell was merely added to over the next 20 years. Jackson is the only President in the 19th century to need two large services of glassware in four years; breakage must have been enormous.

Veron also supplied the White House with a set of French porcelain. It was the first new state dinner service to be ordered since Monroe's in 1817. The service was decorated with the same eagle, shield, and motto as Monroe's service, but the design was reversed.

The Jackson-pattern glassware remaining in the White House now includes two compotes (fig. 5), one small wineglass (figs. 7, 8), four medium wineglasses (fig. 8), five quart decanters—four with handles and one without (fig. 8)—12 water bottles (fig. 8), two wineglass coolers (fig. 9), and six large and three small celery vases (fig. 9). The two compotes are probably the smaller of the "Elegant Center Bowl and Stands" ordered in 1829. The quart decanters, with and without handles, and the water bottles are probably from the 1833 order, which included 18 quart

"Our Federal Union—
it must be preserved,"
proclaims Jackson,
his glass raised in salute.
The President's now
famous reply came during
a Washington banquet
on April 30, 1830. Backers
of a plan to nullify a federal
protective tariff opposed
by South Carolina gave 24
toasts flavored with
states' rights sentiment.
Jackson's simple retort
rallied public opinion to his
position and strengthened
the Union.

decanters without handles, a dozen with handles, and 48 water bottles. Six celery vases were purchased in 1829. Six large ones remain in the White House, but an identical one was purchased by The Corning Museum of Glass several years ago. Two of the quart decanters from this set are in the collection of the Hayes Presidential Center. We would not ordinarily think of this paneled and engraved glass as "richest cut"—the adjective used to describe the pattern on the Bakewell invoice. Previously that description had been reserved for pieces with elaborate diamond cutting. Only the 1829 order included center bowls, however, so it seems certain that this paneled set is the one first ordered by Jackson in 1829.

The three smaller celery vases are of a shape and size normally called "spoonholders" in the mid-19th century. In the White House inventory they are always called "celery vases." In fact, spoonholders were not used for formal dining in elegant circles. They are thus rare in cut glass, though common in the cheaper pressed glass. None of the remaining invoices show any purchase of spoonholders. Wineglass coolers remained in common use to cool and rinse wineglasses between courses, although they became unfashionable later in the century when each guest began to have a number of glasses at his place, one for each wine to be served.

The last of the glassware associated with Jackson in the White House collection is a traveling liquor chest—a wooden box with four decanters in fitted compartments (fig. 10). It was given about 1850 to an ancestor of the donor from someone who had received the set from Jackson. We do not know whether the liquor chest was used in the White House; it may have been purchased by Jackson as a gift or as one of his personal possessions. Decorated with arch and sheaf motifs, it dates in style from before 1845, the year of Jackson's death. The set most likely was purchased from Bakewell, Page and Bakewell, Jackson's preferred glass company. The arch

(Continued on page 44)

and sheaf motifs, commonly used in the 1820s and 1830s, are found on other pieces attributed to Bakewell. The set is one of very few 19th-century ones with a probable American origin. The cutting is much more elaborate than that usually found on liquor-chest decanters, although it is not so elaborate as that on Madison's decanters.

Martin Van Buren

Martin Van Buren, who succeeded Jackson in March 1837, entered a more elaborately finished mansion than had any of his predecessors. Jackson had spent $45,000 on the house during his two terms, leaving it well furnished.

Even so, Congress voted Van Buren a furniture fund of $20,000.[76] Although an inventory of the house was taken March 3, 1837, it has not been located. There is thus no way to know how much of Jackson's glassware remained. Van Buren spent most of his money in refurbishing and repairs, and in 1838 and 1840 he asked for more. Pennsylvania Congressman Charles Ogle seized the opportunity to greatly exaggerate Van Buren's expenditures. The record of Ogle's charges includes a listing of most of the furnishings bought since Monroe's term,[77] providing a cross-check of the glass purchases between 1817 and 1840.

FIG. 7. Wineglasses, left to right: glass probably from the Pierce set, 1853; glass probably first ordered by the Polks, 1845–49; two glasses from the set first ordered by Jackson in 1829. The three at right must have been used together in the 1840s. (Glass on left a gift to the White House collection from Mrs. Daniel C. Digges and Miss Mary Ann Forsyth, 1909; purchased by their grandparents at a White House sale in the 1850s.)

LEFT: FIG. 8. Decanters, water bottle, and wineglasses from the service originally ordered by Jackson from Bakewell, Page and Bakewell in 1829, which was reordered in 1833 and later. Ht. of tallest decanter 15$^5/_8$".

ABOVE: FIG. 9. Two celery vases and wineglass cooler with wineglass from the Jackson service originally ordered in 1829. Celery vases were reordered in 1842; wineglass coolers were bought in 1837 and 1846. Ht. of tallest 10$^1/_4$".

ABOVE: FIG. 10. *Traveling liquor set with four decanters, given by Jackson to a friend before 1845. Probably Bakewell, Page and Bakewell, ca. 1815–35. Ht. of tallest 10". (Gift to the White House collection in 1970 from Russell Wetmore, who had received them from his cousin Harriet V. Wetmore. She was the granddaughter of William C. Wetmore, who had received the set from Jackson's friend about 1850.)*

RIGHT: FIG. 11. *Wineglasses probably ordered in 1845 and later to supplement the Jackson-pattern set. United States. Ht. 5". Both glasses were probably purchased by President and Mrs. Polk.*

(Continued from page 39)

Martin Van Buren was a widower, and his hostess was Angelica Singleton Van Buren, who had married his son in November 1837. The President was fond of entertaining, and his "charming little dinners"[78] were much admired. Ogle, the critical Congressman, had certainly been to several dinners at the President's House.

Van Buren used Jackson's new set of French porcelain during his own term, but he found it necessary to supplement the glassware and ordered more soon after his inauguration. He purchased from James P. Drummond of New York, "Importer and Dealer in China, Glass and Earthenware," 274 pieces of glass for $220.75.[79] A sophisticated New Yorker, Van Buren was probably already familiar with Drummond's store. He received, on June 8, 1837,

6 qt. barrel shape all fluted decanters, cone stopper	*@ $7.00 each*
12 pt. [barrel shape all fluted decanters, cone stopper]	*@ $3.50 [each]*
6 doz. claret wines, cut pillar stem	*@ $7.00 per dozen*
6 doz. green finger cups	*@ $3.66 [per dozen]*
6 doz. cut wine coolers	*@ $9.00 [per dozen]*
2 doz. champagnes	*@ $9.00 [per dozen]*
18 pt. water bottles, flint and fluted	*@ $1.11 each*

The water bottles were subsequently returned for credit. The green finger cups are the first colored glass listed in any White House order. No special cutting or engraving is mentioned, but the prices are about the same as those in the Veron order during the Jackson administration. An exception is the green glass finger cups, so inexpensive that they were probably plain.

In September, 33 dozen glass dishes were bought for $36.[80] In that quantity the dishes must have been intended for use at large White House receptions. They were probably pressed glass—apparently the first pressed glass to be used at the President's House. For the next two decades, in addition, pressed-glass tumblers were purchased in small quantities for family and/or servant use. In 1838 President Van Buren bought six dozen rich-cut tumblers at seven dollars a dozen, and in February 1839, two dozen more.[81] These tumblers were all purchased from Thomas Pursell, a Georgetown merchant, and may have matched the cut pillar stem glasses from Drummond or the tumblers in the Veron order of 1833. On February 26, 1841, Van Buren ordered assorted china and glassware from Hugh Smith & Co., merchants of Alexandria, Virginia. The glassware included "6 doz. Best Cut High flute tumblers" and "4 doz. Best Cut Wine Glasses."[82]

Ogle blustered on for several days in a speech criticizing the President's spending. He wrongly accused Van Buren of buying Jackson's glass sets of 1829 and 1833, as well as the smaller amount of glass he had purchased from Drummond:

I will direct your attention for a few minutes to the magnificent set of Table Glass contained in three several [separate] bills. The first bill is for Champagne Glasses, Clarets, Goblets, Cordials, Water Bottles, &c. bought from Messrs. Veron & Co. . . . The second bill is . . . purchased from Bakewell & Co. . . . The third bill . . . was rendered by James P. Drummond. . . . These three bills for table glass make the clever sum of $2,956.50. What will honest Loco Focos say to Mr. van Buren for spending the People's cash in foreign Fanny Kemble green finger cups, in which to wash his pretty tapering, soft, white lily fingers after dining on fricandeau de veau and omelette souffle?

How will the friends of temperance relish the foreign "cut wine coolers" and the "barrel shape flute decanters with cone stoppers"?[83]

Quite possibly Ogle accused Van Buren of buying foreign glass simply to make the President appear snobbish.

The deep green finger bowls were a new fashion in the mid-thirties. From then until the 1850s it was stylish to use green or blue finger bowls with colorless stemware on the table. The bowls usually were not cut or engraved. One housewife's advice book of the period described their use, under the listing "finger glasses":

These are generally blue or green, and are filled with water and set round the table, just before the cloth is removed, for the company to dip their fingers in, rubbing them with a slice of lemon or an orange leaf, that is put into each glass for the purpose.[84]

Van Buren owned a personal set of English table glass, bought for him in England in June 1839 by his son John.[85] This glass was paid for by the President, and he probably took it home with him when he left Washington. According to the invoice for the set, there were two dozen each of six sizes of stemware, all engraved in Queens pattern, plus water carafes, wineglass coolers, and four quart-size decanters. No finger bowls of any color are mentioned. The glass cost £62 for 200 items (about $300 at that time). Since it was more expensive than the set Van Buren had chosen for the White House, it probably had much more elaborately cut decoration.

William Henry Harrison and John Tyler

The next President, William Henry Harrison, died only a month after taking office. He did not buy any glassware during his brief term. Vice President John Tyler succeeded him. President Tyler placed glass orders several times, but all the purchases were small ones. His orders from Thomas Pursell included

June 8, 1841	4 doz rich cut wines	$22.00
Aug. 14, [1841]	3 doz. glass cup plates	$ 2.25
Sept. 30	1 doz. green finger bowls	$ 5.00
Dec. 10	1 doz. rich cut tumblers	$ 6.00
[Dec. 10]	1 doz. Pressed tumblers	$ 3.50
Dec. 14	1 doz. Press [tumblers]	$ 3.50
Jan. 29, 1842	2 pair cut cellery glasses	$10.00
June 21	4 doz. tumblers	$15.50
June 30	2 doz plain tumblers	$ 1.00
July 10	2 doz. plain tumblers	$ 2.00
Jan. 11, 1844	4 doz. rich cut flint tumblers	$20.00
	1 doz. green finger bowls	$ 5.00
Jan. 3, 1845	2$\frac{1}{2}$ doz. cut flint tumblers	$11.25[86]

It seems likely that some of these items augmented the glassware sets bought by Jackson and supplemented by Van Buren. The cut tumblers that had been $20 a dozen in 1829 had dropped to five or six dollars a dozen in 1842. The lower costs probably reflected the growth that had taken place in the American glass industry, leading to increased availability of good glassware. However, the lower prices might have

First Chief Executive born under the U. S. flag, Martin Van Buren served as Jackson's Vice President. He gained the White House by popular vote in the election of 1836. Apparently, Van Buren purchased the first pressed glassware to be used in the White House, 33 dozen dishes. The dishes represented a new technology, machine-pressing of glass, America's most important contribution to the glass industry.

DETAIL OF PORTRAIT BY GEORGE P. A. HEALY, WHITE HOUSE COLLECTION indicated that the tumblers and other cheaper items had not been engraved with the coat of arms of the United States.

The pressed tumblers, which had only recently become available with new technology, cost about half as much as the cut ones. The plain tumblers, at a dollar a dozen, and the pressed cup plates, at 75 cents a dozen, were even cheaper. This is the only record of cup plates in the White House. Cup plates were used to hold teacups for tea drinkers who were sipping the beverage from their saucers—a not uncommon custom, but considered unfashionable in the best circles. The lack of other cup plate records is evidence that these items were not used on formal occasions.

John Tyler's first wife died during his Presidency. Until his remarriage most of his dinners were presided over by his daughter, Letitia Tyler Semple, and his daughter-in-law, Priscilla Tyler. Priscilla has left several descriptions of White House social affairs in her letters to her sister. In this letter, she describes an especially elegant ball she organized for the French Marshal Bertrand:

> *Father, with his usual kindness, had given me a carte-blanche . . . and my supper was splendid (it is so easy to entertain at other people's expense). The prettiest things on the table were two pyramids composed of pomegranates with the skins peeled off and Malaga grapes. They looked like rubies and emeralds. I had quantities of vases of natural flowers down the table, and festoons of grapes going from vase to vase the whole length of the table, which of course was covered with everything possible in the way of jellies, ices, creams, &c, &c, and quantities of the most beautiful French bonbons. Nothing was on the long principal table but things of the most glittering description. Meats were all banished to the side table. . . .*[87]

James K. Polk

President Polk succeeded Tyler in March 1845, and he and his wife redecorated. They had gas lighting installed in 1848 and purchased a carpet especially woven with the American eagle in the design.[88] Apparently, they found the glassware sadly depleted. In April 1845 they bought from Baldwin Gardiner of New York, for $124, three and a half dozen cut goblets; four dozen each of cut champagne glasses, wineglasses, and liquor glasses; and a pair of claret decanters.[89]

More glass was bought on May 24 from Ebenezer Collamore. At $40.50 for 15 dozen items, it was less than half the price of the Gardiner order. There were five dozen cut hocks, six dozen straw stem wines (a "straw stem" is a delicate straight stem), and four dozen straw stem clarets.[90] Together the two orders would provide a dinner service for 48 people. It is odd that the glass was not all obtained from the same merchant, though, for the orders were placed only a month apart. There is no suggestion that these are special orders, and no engraving is mentioned. The low prices of the Collamore pieces may indicate that they were made in Europe of non-lead glass. Ebenezer Collamore, a New York City retailer of china, glass, and earthenware from 1832 until 1860, handled both domestic and imported goods.[91]

The following year the Polks bought more glass from B. Gardiner, including three dozen cut-glass goblets and wines, two dozen cut-glass champagnes and green finger bowls, and a dozen cut-glass wineglass coolers.[92] The only serving pieces ordered were decanters, perhaps because Jackson's serving pieces were still in use.

Mrs. Polk's niece, Joanna Rucker, accompanied the Polks to Washington for a lengthy visit. Her letters to her cousin Bet in Tennessee provide a picture of life in the White House. The easy public access to the President and his family is shown in her accounts of their evening receptions. Of one reception she wrote:

> *Last night was reception night, . . . there are two nights in the week that is set apart for company, and everyone that wishes comes to the White House to spend the evening. Some of the ladies dress in party dress; others wear bonnets and shawls, and I tell you it is amusing to see the contrast.*[93]

The lack of privacy endured by the first family was apparent in another of her letters:

> *I have just been disturbed by a straggler through the hall. He pretended to miss his way in going from the President's office and came down in the private part of the hall into the parlor. There is but little privacy here as the house belongs to the Government and everyone feels at home. They sometimes stalk into our bedrooms and say they are looking at the house!*[94]

FIG. 12. The engraved insignia on the left wineglass in figure 11. "Out of many, one," says the Latin inscription on the scroll decorating this emblem of the mid-1800s. The country's motto alludes to the merger of the 13 original colonies into an indivisible Union.

Sarah Polk was an intellectual who served as her husband's able secretary as well as his hostess. The couple had no children; Sarah devoted herself to her husband's career. For religious reasons she did not permit dancing at White House parties, and she substituted wine for whiskey punch at receptions. Nonetheless, she entertained her guests elegantly—including the aged Dolley Madison, who lived nearby. Sarah Polk held Tuesday and Friday drawing rooms as well as frequent dinner parties. A fairly detailed account survives of one of these dinners, but the description of glassware in it is more confusing than helpful. Mrs. J. E. Dixon, wife of one of the Connecticut senators, was invited to dinner at five o'clock on December 19, 1845. She found herself in the company of the Supreme Court justices and their wives, the attorney general and his wife, and the members of the Judiciary Committee and their wives, a group of about 40 guests. She reported:

> *The dinner table was as handsome as any I ever saw in proportion to its size, not even excepting the supper table at the Tuilleries at the Queen's Ball. . . . There were two hundred chandeliers, candelabras and figures around the grand center ornament, all of which were of gilt burnished and very brilliant with vases of flowers. . . . Sit! I guess we did sit—for four mortal hours, I judge one hundred fifty courses for everything was in the French style and each dish a separate course. Soup, fish, green peas, spinach, canvas back duck, turkey, birds, oyster pies, cotolettes di mouton, ham deliciously garnished, potatoes like snowballs, croquettes poulet in various forms, duck and olives, pate de foie gras, jellies, orange and lemon charlotte Russe, ices and "pink mud" oranges, prunes, sweetmeats, mottos and everything one can imagine, all served in silver dishes with silver tureens and wine coolers and the famous gold forks, knives and spoons for dessert. The china was white and gold and blue with a crest, the eagle of course, and the dessert plates were marine blue and gold with a painting in the center of fruits and flowers. The President had to be so kind as to drink all our healths, although we looked in a pretty case just then. The glass ware was very handsome, blue & white, finely cut, and pink champagne, gold sherry, green hock, maderia, the ruby port and sauterne formed a rainbow round each plate with the finger glasses and water decanters. . . . Coffee was served and liquors and we adieu and reach home at ten o'clock.*[95]

By pushing a foot treadle, a glass engraver powers his lathe. Touching a vase to a spinning copper wheel, the engraver abrades a pattern into the glass. Engraving yields designs more delicate and intricate than glass cutting can achieve. America's first engraved glass of excellence came from the factory of John F. Amelung, a German immigrant who set up shop near Frederick, Maryland, in 1784.

REPRODUCED FROM *CURIOSITIES OF GLASSMAKING*, BY APSLEY PELLATT, LONDON, 1849

Mrs. Dixon seems to describe blue and white glassware finely cut. At this time, however, colored *cut* glassware was not yet fashionable. Furthermore, the orders for the Polk administration already cited indicate that nothing but undecorated finger bowls were colored (though an inventory taken in 1849 [see below] lists green wine-glasses). In saying "blue and white glassware," Mrs. Dixon may have meant plain blue glassware—perhaps finger bowls—and colorless, finely cut glassware. That would certainly describe the surviving glass with its engraved coat of arms.

The following year the Polks ordered the first new porcelain dinner service since Jackson's set of 1833, selecting French porcelain from Alexander Stewart & Co. of New York City. The service had a shield with stars and stripes on the rim, but no eagle—a design slightly less flamboyant than the previous one.

The first White House inventory since 1825 to survive was taken during the Polk administration. Dated January 1, 1849, it lists

47 water glasses	10 Jelly glasses
62 Champagne glasses	2 Cellery glasses
71 wine glasses	40 Water-Bottles
39 glass wine coolers	18 Wine Decanters, very old
32 small size wine coolers	4 Claret-Decanters, good
28 Claret glasses	6 Liquor glasses, old
42 Finger Bowls	5 Punch glasses, old
12 Ice Glasses	1 Plated stand with 3 Liquor Bottles
38 wine glasses, green	1 Water-Pitcher, glass[96]
32 Claret glasses	
40 Champagne glasses, long	

The inventory includes many pieces that can be matched to the surviving engraved Jackson-pattern pieces ordered by Jackson or his successors. The most mysterious items on the inventory are the "38 wine glasses, green." These engraved glasses (figs. 7, 11), still in the White House collection, appear on every subsequent inventory. However, they are not to be found on any of the orders of the 1830s and 1840s, unless they are Mrs. Polk's hock glasses bought in 1845. Hock glasses were traditionally green, but Mrs. Polk's were so inexpensive it is difficult to believe they were specially engraved. There are 41 green glasses in the collection today, so if most of these were Mrs. Polk's hock glasses, either the inventory was incorrectly counted or more green glasses were purchased afterward.

Of the surviving green glasses, all have the grapevine design similar to that on the Jackson service, and all but two have an insignia identical to that on the colorless glass (fig. 12). The plain straight stems of these glasses are similar to the stems on several vintage-engraved glasses in two sizes, which were probably ordered to match the Jackson service. These may be Mrs. Polk's straw stem wines. There are only a few of these left in the White House. Like the green wines, they must represent at least two orders, since there are differences in the engraving (figs. 13, 14).

Green finger bowls turn up in four orders, but none appear on an inventory or remain today. All together, 120 green finger bowls were ordered between 1837 and 1845, but by 1849 none were in use. There are 71 wineglass coolers in two sizes, probably from Van Buren's order in 1837 and the Polks' purchase in 1846, and 42 finger bowls (some of which *might* have been green).

The 18 old wine decanters must be a mixture of Jackson's and later orders; no sizes or types are given. There are three surviving pint decanters, cut and engraved

White House hosts President and Mrs. James K. Polk (center) gather with guests: Secretary of State James Buchanan (far left), his niece Harriet Lane (next to Buchanan), Dolley Madison (next to Polk), and others. Before Polk left office in 1849 the U. S. flag waved from coast to coast. During Polk's Presidency a shield with stars and stripes embellished a new porcelain dinner service— the first to be ordered since Jackson's term.

to match the Jackson service, but none are still in the White House. One was acquired in the antiques market by the Corning Museum of Glass in 1983 (fig. 18); another was part of the glassware taken to Ohio by the Hayeses in 1881; a third was given to Ethel Roosevelt near the time her father left office in 1909. Pint decanters were ordered in 1829 and 1837; judging by their shape, they seem more likely to date from 1837. The surviving decanters differ in one respect: Two of them have a paneled ring around the neck below the mouth, whereas the third has a diamond-faceted ring. A fourth pint decanter of the same shape, but with a slightly different insignia and cutting, has a faceted neck ring (figs. 17, 18). Probably the last remnant of one of these orders, it is in the collection of the Hayes Presidential Center.

The 40 water bottles must be ones purchased by Jackson. No tumblers appear on the list, reflecting Mrs. Polk's decision to replace whiskey punch with wine at her receptions. The last tumbler orders date from Tyler's term. The 47 water glasses could be those tumblers that survived, or they could be stemmed water goblets.

Among the glass pieces in the White House collection associated with the Polks are an English finger bowl and glass (fig. 15). Both pieces, gifts to the White House in the early 20th century, are blue trimmed with white. They may have been used in the White House by the Polks, but they were personal possessions that probably pre-date his Presidency.

Another early 20th-century gift to the White House—also colored glass—is a green decanter from the 1830s or 1840s (fig. 15). Said to have been purchased at a White House sale in the mid-19th century, it has no association with a particular administration. The decanter is lead glass. Since no American glass of this color has been documented so early, it was probably made in England. A fourth piece given to the White House in this century is an engraved *(Continued on page 58)*

*Opponent of hard liquor,
First Lady Sarah Polk substituted
wine for whiskey punch. She
entertained dutifully. During one
dinner that lasted four hours,
glasses of different wines "formed
a rainbow around each plate,"
wrote a senator's wife.*

DETAIL OF PORTRAIT BY GEORGE P. A. HEALY,
JAMES K. POLK ANCESTRAL HOME, COLUMBIA, TENNESSEE

*ABOVE: FIG. 13. Wineglass, probably ordered 1845–60 to supplement
the Jackson or Pierce set. Ht. 4$^1/_2$".*

*RIGHT: FIG. 14. Wineglasses, probably bought 1845–60 to supplement
the Jackson or Pierce set. Ht. of taller 4$^1/_2$". These glasses and the
ones in figure 13 are nonlead glass and may be European. The top
rims have been ground down to smooth away chips.*

LEFT: *FIG. 15. Decanter, glass, and finger bowl, probably English, 1820–40. Decanter ht. 12". (Decanter a gift to the White House collection in 1918 from Mrs. Charles W. Richardson, whose mother purchased it at a White House sale in the 19th century. Finger bowl and glass owned by President and Mrs. Polk; a gift, in 1907, of Mrs. George M. Fall, Mrs. Polk's niece.)*

ABOVE: *FIG. 16. Decanter and glasses owned by President and Mrs. Zachary Taylor. United States, 1830–50. Ht. of decanter 11³/₄". (Gift to the White House collection, in 1915, from the children of Capt. John Taylor Wood, a grandson of the Taylors.)*

ABOVE: FIG. 17. The engraved insignia on the decanter on the left in figure 18.

RIGHT: FIG. 18. Pint decanters, probably ordered in 1837 and later to supplement the Jackson-pattern set. United States. Ht. of taller 14$^1/_4$". The decanter on the left had a stopper probably identical to the one in the decanter on the right. The necks of both originally extended above the collars.

LEFT: FIG. 19. *Finger bowl, claret glass, and dessert-wine glass, probably ordered in 1849, 1850, or 1853 to supplement the Jackson-pattern set. United States. Ht. of claret glass $4^3/_4''$.*

ABOVE: FIG. 20. *Ashburton pattern cut wineglass, used in the White House in the mid-19th century. United States, 1844–52. Ht. $4^3/_{16}''$.*

RIGHT: FIG. 21. *Decanter, used in the White House in the mid-19th century. Probably Bohemian, 1830–50. Ht. $9^5/_8''$. (Figures 20 and 21, gifts to the White House collection from Mrs. Daniel C. Digges and Miss Mary Ann Forsyth, 1909; originally purchased by their grandparents at a White House sale in the 1850s.)*

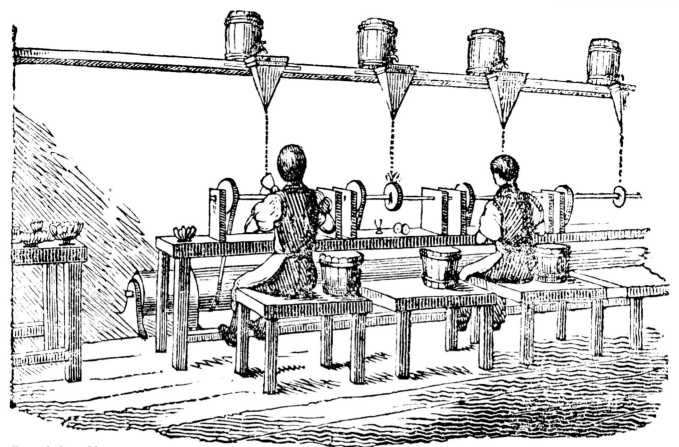

Funnel-shaped hoppers drip an abrasive solution of sand and water onto revolving wheels in a depiction of the glass-cutting process. Artisans hold glassware against the spinning wheels to cut deep or shallow grooves. A buffing wheel gives the design its final polish. The process of glass cutting was known as early as the seventh century B. C., possibly earlier.

(Continued from page 49) decanter—probably Bohemian—which might possibly be one of those purchased from Drummond or from Gardiner. Because it is a non-lead glass, this decanter is certainly continental (fig. 21). It too supposedly came from a mid-century White House sale.

Zachary Taylor

President Taylor, hero of the Mexican War, was in office for slightly more than a year before he died. Records of only a few purchases of glass survive from that time. Four dozen rose-colored clarets were bought on May 30, 1849, for seven dollars a dozen from C. S. Fowler, a Washington retailer.[97] Fowler sold the White House 23 cut goblets in November and 13 Ashburton goblets the following month, along with half a dozen finger bowls.[98]

The Ashburton goblets, at 44 cents apiece, were probably cut glass rather than pressed. The finger bowls, judging from their price of 27 cents each, were probably plain. The Ashburton pattern was named after Alexander Baring, Lord Ashburton, one of the most popular English diplomats ever to come to the United States. Ashburton negotiated a boundary dispute between the United States and Canada. Daniel Webster, Secretary of State, took part in the negotiations, which resulted in the Webster-Ashburton Treaty of 1842. The Ashburton pattern, most common in pressed glass, was made in a multitude of shapes by many companies. It was a simple pattern with large facets that imitated the fashionable panel cutting. Occasionally, the pattern was executed in cut glass, although that was more expensive.

Another 13 Ashburton goblets were bought January 24, along with eight dozen wineglasses for $3.25 a dozen, again from Fowler.[99] On January 29 a pair of pitchers was purchased, and on February 6, 41 hock glasses were purchased for seven dollars a dozen.[100] In such large numbers, the wine and hock glasses must have been for entertaining. The smaller quantities were apparently for family use. Thomas Pursell was still supplying the White House with glass; on December 11, 1849, he sold Colonel Bliss, the purchasing agent, six cut-glass decanters for two dollars each.[101]

Among the glassware in the White House collection donated by descendants of the Presidents is a colorless panel-cut decanter with two matching wineglasses and a jelly glass—all four pieces (fig. 16) said to have been used by the Taylors. The glass, simple in design, would have been in keeping with the relatively Spartan style of General and Mrs. Taylor. The four pieces do not form a set. The decanter is made of nonlead glass; the wineglasses and jelly glass are of lead glass. The Taylors probably owned these before Zachary Taylor's election. One other gift to the collection associated with Taylor's administration is a wineglass cut in the Ashburton pattern (fig. 20), supposedly purchased at a White House sale in the 1850s.

Millard Fillmore

Taylor died in office in July 1850 and was succeeded by his Vice President, Millard Fillmore. In November of that year Fillmore bought "3 Rich Mitre Cut Water Bottles" from Fowler[102] as well as a dozen each of ruby finger bowls and dark blue finger bowls from Davis Collamore.[103] The ruby bowls cost twice as much as the blue ones, suggesting that the ruby ones might have been cut or engraved. Pursell supplied 18 more cut-glass decanters for three dollars each in December,[104] but the White House went back to Fowler the same month for a dozen cut saltcellars, a dozen cut cordials, two cake covers, a dozen hock glasses, 13 wineglasses, and a dozen water bottles.[105] Late in 1851 Fowler supplied two dozen each of cut champagne glasses, wineglasses, and cordials at $7.50, $7.00, and $6.50 a dozen.[106] It is likely that most of these were cut or engraved to match previous purchases.

Two sales of discarded White House furnishings took place during the 1850s, on November 22, 1851, and on April 22, 1852.[107] No lists were kept of these sales, but some of the glass from the 1849 inventory was probably sold.

Some of the rose claret glasses bought in 1849 by Taylor and the ruby finger bowls bought in 1850 by Fillmore are still in the White House, along with a few smaller rose-colored wineglasses (fig. 19). The smaller glasses were intended for a dessert wine. The stems of the wineglasses are colorless, but their bowls are rose colored. The wineglass bowls are made of two layers: colorless glass lined with colored glass. The finger bowls too are twin-layered—some ruby, others rose. The pieces are engraved with grape leaves, vines, and an insignia (fig. 22) that matches the one on the Jackson-pattern service and on the green wineglasses purchased in the 1840s. Laurel leaves and palm fronds—no arrows—are clustered near the eagle's talons.

The finger bowls seem to have been ordered at least twice, for 13 rose ones and six ruby ones remain in the collection. There is also a rose one at the Hayes Presidential Center. At least one rose claret glass, apparently sold from the White House in the 1890s, is owned by a private collector. In all, not many rose-colored wineglasses seem to have been ordered. They do not appear in pictures of the table taken in the 1880s, so by that time they had been retired.

Franklin Pierce

Franklin Pierce took office in March 1853, and he received an appropriation of $25,000 for his furniture fund.[108] From this he bought new services of porcelain and

FIG. 22. The engraved insignia on the larger wineglass in figure 19. The stylized glassware shield, like the one on the Great Seal, displays 13 vertical stripes. The stripes on the seal derived from the U. S. flag, which the Continental Congress authorized in 1777.

glass. Although the President and his wife were in mourning for their 11-year-old son, who had been killed in a railroad accident two months earlier, they continued to entertain. Custom dictated weekly morning and evening receptions while Congress was in session; the Pierces also gave weekly formal dinners for 36 guests.[109]

President Pierce ordered both china and glassware for the White House following his visit to the New York Crystal Palace Exhibition on July 14, 1853. Probably he had seen a china service displayed there by the New York retailers Haughwout & Dailey. A contemporary illustration shows two plates that Haughwout stated had been prepared by his firm for the President. One of the plates contains an eagle, a shield, and a motto; the second plate has a simpler design of a shield with an initial *P*. Pierce ordered the simple set for the White House, but with a blank shield. Perhaps he felt that heraldic china smacked of the aristocracy. The set was French porcelain, decorated at Haughwout's atelier.[110] What glassware Pierce may have seen at Haughwout's exhibit is unknown; but according to the exhibition catalog, the firm also displayed cut glassware.[111] The President ordered a service of cut glass along with the china.

That the Haughwout company employed glass cutters during the late 1840s and the 1850s is known. Talented glasscutters John Hoare, an Englishman, and John S. O'Connor, an Irishman, both worked for the firm during those years. Haughwout's glass cutting may have been done in Brooklyn, probably on the premises of the Brooklyn Flint Glass Company, since Haughwout listed "Brooklyn Cut Glass" on its billhead in later years.[112] Furthermore, no address for the Haughwout cutting shop appears in Brooklyn directories of the time. John Hoare left Haughwout & Dailey in 1853 to found his own cutting shop, which subsequently went through several partnerships. By 1857 it was called Hoare & Dailey (Joseph Dailey, his last partner, was a glasscutter; he may also have been related to Haughwout's partner). Hoare & Dailey was located on the premises of the Brooklyn Flint Glass Company on State Street. Thus Hoare might have continued to work for Haughwout, perhaps as a subcontractor rather than as an employee.

The glassware service ordered by Pierce was very large and cost more than the porcelain, though both served 60 people. The glass cost $801.87; the porcelain, $536.24.[113] Some secondhand glass and china was turned in to Haughwout & Dailey to reduce the cost. A credit of $180.11 was allowed, but the used goods were not itemized on the invoice. The glassware included

5 Doz Goblets	*$10.37 per doz.*
5 Doz Champagnes	*$ 8.25 [per doz.]*
4 [Doz] Finger Bowls	*$18.00 [per doz.]*
5 Doz Pomona Green Hocks	*$ 5.50 [per doz.]*
5 [Doz] Ruby Clarets	*$14.75 [per doz.]*
5 Doz. Irving Wines	*$ 4.00 [per doz.]*
5 [Doz.] Lammartine Wines	*$ 3.75 [per doz.]*
5 [Doz.] Hocks	*$ 5.50 [per doz.]*
5 [Doz.] Eng. Wines	*$ 6.50 [per doz.]*
4 Doz Wine Coolers	*$ 15.00 [per doz.]*
4 Doz Cordials	*$ 6.00 [per doz.]*
4 [Doz.] Lemonades	*$ 8.25 [per doz.]*
4 [Doz.] Water Bottles	*$38.00 [per doz.]*
6 Pr. Qt Decanters	*$10.00 [per pr.]*
6 Pr. Pint Decanters	*$ 8.00 per pr.*

2 Doz Han'd Flaggons	*$12.50 [per doz.]*
1 Pr. Celerys	*$16.00*
3 pr salts	*$ 2.50 [per pr.]*
2 Pr. Ice Bowls	*$ 5.50 [per pr.]*

No pattern is listed on the above order, and some of the terms are unclear. The prices for the goblets, champagnes, and ruby clarets seem nearly comparable. The green glass is much cheaper, probably because it was not cut. The finger bowls and wineglass coolers, on the other hand, are surprisingly expensive. "Irving" and "Lammartine" might be pattern designations, but if so, one wonders why the names do not appear in the entries for the other shapes.

Nineteenth-century rules for table setting are of little help in identifying the glasses listed. Said Miss Leslie:

> *At the right hand of every plate place a tumbler, and one or more wine-glasses, according to the variety of wines that are to be brought to the table; it being customary to drink different wines out of different sorts of glasses; the fashionable glass for each wine varying so frequently, that it is difficult in this respect to give any rules. The decanters are to stand near the corners. It is now usual at many tables to have a small water-bottle (holding about a pint) placed by the side of every plate, that each person may pour out water for himself.[114]*

Given the size of Pierce's set, it is surprising that Fowler supplied a pair of cut-glass dishes in December.[115] Moreover, several cut-glass goblets and tumblers were purchased from Boteler at the same time.[116]

It is impossible to identify the Pierce service with any certainty today. Despite its size, very little probably remains. The Jackson coat-of-arms service is the only large pre-1860 service in the White House collection. Unless the Pierces were merely supplementing Jackson's service, their glass could not have been the Jackson paneled service, for they did not order center bowls, claret decanters, or more than two celeries. The handled flagons—wine or water pitchers—cannot be claret decanters; they are much cheaper than the quart decanters. Since Pierce chose not to order the porcelain service with the American eagle and shield prepared by Haughwout, it is unlikely that he would have chosen a glass service with that engraving.

The White House collection, however, has remnants of a cut and engraved service that includes a few water carafes that have been in the mansion since their purchase in the 19th century, as well as a decanter, a wineglass cooler, and a wineglass acquired separately in the 20th century—all bought at one of the White House sales (fig. 23). These may be remnants of Pierce's service, since they do not match any of the purchases of the 1840s. Perhaps, because this service had no insignia, it lost its identification in White House records soon after its purchase, and the pieces sold to the public during the second half of the 19th century became similarly anonymous.

A few months after the Haughwout order, it was decided to send President Monroe's magnificent French gilded bronze and glass plateau (fig. 24) to Philadelphia for resilvering of the mirror. At the same time, more china and glass were purchased. New glass liners for silver saltcellars were bought, along with "2 large cut Jelly Glasses" for $42 and "32 smaller [cut jelly glasses] for Plateau" for $118.[117] The two large cut jelly glasses are actually compote bowls, which can be seen in early photographs sitting on the plateau. The smaller ones purchased for the plateau,

Stacks smoking at full capacity, New York's Brooklyn Flint Glass Company appears as a line engraving in an advertisement in The Home Journal, *March 20, 1852. Between 1800 and 1837 more than a hundred glasshouses had sprung up to supply a country expanding westward.*

which fit on figures holding them aloft, are also still in the White House collection (fig. 24, inset). They might be English or American glass; it is impossible to tell. An account describing the plateau as it looked a few years later mentioned its adornments. The "small crystal dishes" were the small jelly glasses:

> *Mr. Buchanan set an example of Republican simplicity. . . . The dinner table was not ornamented with flowers nor were bouquets at the covers. A long plateau, a mirror edged with a hunting scene (gilt figures in high relief) extended down the middle, and from the centre and at the two ends rose epergnes with small crystal dishes for bonbons and cakes.[118]*

James Buchanan

James Buchanan was a bachelor when he took office, so his niece Harriet Lane acted as his hostess. Buchanan had been a diplomat in London, and the popular Miss Lane had served as his hostess there. At 27 she was already experienced in running a large household when her uncle became President. Buchanan was determined not to overspend his furniture allowance, and he made that plain to Harriet. In a letter to her dated May 20, 1858, he wrote: ". . . this sum must answer our purpose until the end of my term. I wish you therefore not to expend the whole of it; but to leave enough to meet all contingencies up till 4 March, 1861."[119]

Buchanan made frequent purchases of glassware, but all were comparatively small—obviously replacements for Pierce's service or possibly for Jackson's. He ordered no serving pieces other than several decanters and an ice pitcher. On December 19, 1857, Tyndale and Mitchell sold five dozen straight-barrel and six dozen round-barrel engraved wineglasses to the White House.[120] On December 16 three new bottles for the liquor frame (on the 1849 inventory) were purchased from Bailey & Co. of Philadelphia.[121] On July 22, 1858, four dozen sherry glasses and the same quantity of Madeira glasses, along with two dozen punch glasses, were purchased

ABOVE: Inside a Brooklyn glassworks, a multi-pot furnace heats the pace of production. Workmen inflate gathers of molten glass while young helpers fetch and carry pontils and other tools.

RIGHT: FIG. 23. Wineglass, water carafe, claret decanter, and wineglass cooler, probably from the set ordered by President Franklin Pierce in 1853 from Haughwout & Dailey. Ht. of decanter $11^7/_8"$. (Water carafe in White House since original purchase. Wineglass, gift of Mrs. Daniel C. Digges and Miss Mary Ann Forsyth, 1909; purchased by their grandparents at a White House sale in the 1850s. Decanter and wineglass cooler, gift of the White House Historical Association, 1971; purchased at a mid-1800s White House sale.)

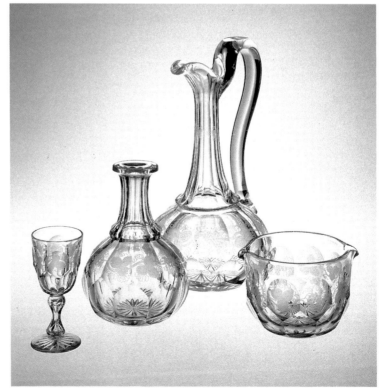

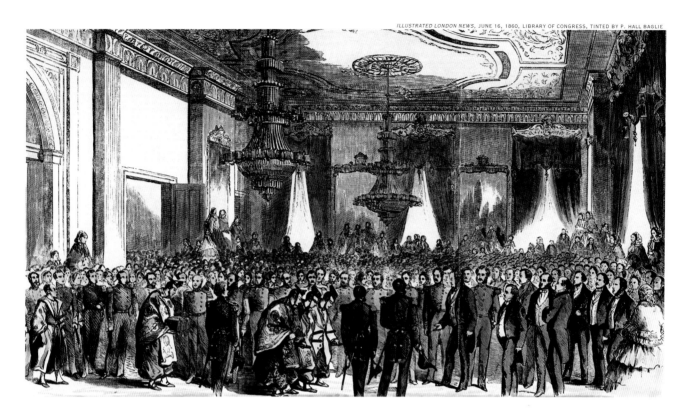

*In 1860 President
Buchanan receives the first
diplomatic entourage to
Washington from imperial
Japan. Americans climbed
on chairs to view the
envoys' Oriental dress and
exotic hairstyles. Harriet
Lane, niece of the bachelor
President, served as
his hostess. She put White
House glassware to use
at sumptuous banquets
and celebrated balls.*

from E. V. Haughwout and Co., successors to Haughwout & Dailey.[122] Charles
Fowler & Co. supplied a half dozen engraved liquors in November 1858 and a dozen
engraved goblets the following month.[123] In July 1859 the White House bought from
C. W. Boteler, the Washington dealer, an ice pitcher, two dozen goblets, and a
dozen wineglasses.[124]

Despite the restrictions on her spending, Harriet gave brilliant dinners and
receptions. Probably the social highlights of Buchanan's term were the separate vis-
its of a group of Japanese envoys and of the Prince of Wales, later Edward VII, both
in 1860. The Japanese envoys caused much excitement; the members of the delega-
tion were the first Japanese most Americans had seen. The prince created an even
greater sensation. Miss Lane arranged two dinner parties so that all the Cabinet
members, senators, and other notables would have a chance to meet him. The President gave a public reception in the East Room to enable more guests to meet the first
member of the British royal family to visit the United States. The prince and Miss
Lane visited Mount Vernon as well, where he paid his respects to the memory of
George Washington. The three-day stay was a triumph for Harriet.

FIG. 24. *President Monroe's French plateau,*
with glass bonbon dishes and centerpieces
added by President Pierce in 1854.

INSET: *The bonbon dishes on the plateau.*

The Lincoln Service

President and Mrs. Lincoln ordered in 1861 the state service that would be in use the longest at the White House. It was reordered at least seven times and supplied by at least four companies during a 40-year span. The service departed from traditional heavy cut glass. It was much thinner, and, in addition to having fine diamond cutting, it had delicately engraved swags. Like the 1829 Jackson service, the Lincoln pattern represented the latest in fashion. The service had an eagle insignia similar to that designed by Haughwout in 1853 for the presidential china and to the coat of arms on the Jackson service. The Lincoln-pattern insignia is enclosed within a shield-shaped cartouche, and the eagle carries arrows in its left talon and an olive branch in its right (fig. 26). The Lincoln-pattern pieces in the White House today include serving pieces, a finger bowl, an ice cream plate, and eight sizes of drinking glasses. A mixture from various orders during different administrations, the pieces have a number of color differences and minor differences in the engraving (figs. 25–33).

FIG. 25. Decanters, water carafe, goblet, and punch glass from the service first ordered by President and Mrs. Abraham Lincoln in 1861 and reordered by his successors through 1902. Ht. of tallest 12".

Abraham Lincoln

When the Lincolns entered the White House early in 1861, Mrs. Lincoln found many of the furnishings inadequate. Despite the war clouds on the horizon, she set about redecorating the mansion. The Lincolns' first reception was held on March 8, just days after the inauguration, and the first state dinner was given on March 28.[125]

That spring, Mrs. Lincoln ordered a new state dinner service to replace Pierce's, as well as a new glassware service. She ordered the porcelain in New York from E. V. Haughwout & Company (successors to Haughwout & Dailey), choosing the service with the American eagle that Pierce had rejected in 1853. She had the color of the rim changed from blue to reddish purple (a color called solferino); otherwise, the design is the same as that on the plate originally submitted for Pierce's approval by Haughwout. The china service cost more than $3,000.[126]

Mrs. Lincoln did not, however, choose the new glassware from Haughwout. That service was ordered through A. P. Zimaudy, a retailer or glass company agent,[127] and it was delivered in July. The copy of the original order is missing from the National Archives. The only remaining documentation is the invoice from

FIG. 26. The engraved insignia on the celery vase in figure 30. The order, placed by Mrs. Lincoln, called for "one sett of Glass Ware rich cut & eng'd with U. S. Coat of Arms." Most of the pieces of this service, initially ordered in 1861, bear an identical insignia.

Zimaudy "For one sett of Glass Ware rich cut & eng'd with U. S. Coat of Arms: $1500."[128] The bill was approved for payment and signed by both the Lincolns.

The china service was intended to serve three to four dozen diners, so the glassware probably had a minimum of four dozen each of at least six shapes of individual pieces and some serving pieces. Since the glass cost nearly twice as much as Pierce's service, it probably had more pieces. On the other hand, Pierce's service was a very simple one, and Mrs. Lincoln's choice was embellished with elaborate copper-wheel engraving, considerably more costly than cutting alone.

The shapes in the Lincoln set may have been similar to those presented by E. V. Haughwout & Company to the Japanese envoys who had visited the United States the previous year. The presentation sets included goblets, champagnes, clarets, wineglasses, green hocks, cordials, quart and pint decanters, claret decanters, center bowls, side dishes, finger bowls, and saltcellars.[129] There are no matching saltcellars in the White House and none on any of the inventories of the 1860s, but the other shapes listed are, or were, in the White House. Mrs. Lincoln's set may have included, in addition, handled punch cups, ice cream plates, water carafes, sugar bowls, and celery vases, since examples of all of these are still in the White House.

The glassware service was apparently ordered by Zimaudy from Christian Dorflinger's newly built Greenpoint Glass Works, in Brooklyn. Dorflinger had learned the glass business in France and had come to the United States in the 1840s. In 1860 he built the Greenpoint Glass Works. It was the third glass factory he was to operate in Brooklyn but the first intended primarily for the manufacture of fine table glass. Although there are no existing records to document the connection between Zimaudy and Dorflinger or confirm that the service was made at Dorflinger's glasshouse, seven factory samples in this pattern have descended in two different branches of the Dorflinger family, with the tradition that they were made at Greenpoint. Because the service was used for so long and reordered so often, we do not know how many of the remaining pieces were part of the first order. Probably few of the surviving stemware pieces date from 1861, but some of the serving pieces may.

The Lincolns gave a state dinner for Prince Napoleon in August 1861,[130] probably the first time the new glassware was used. Among American glass manufacturers the service received a great deal of attention, and several glassmakers claimed to have worked on it. In June 1863 a new glass factory was being built in Portland, Maine. The superintendent, Enoch Egginton, was an English glass cutter who had previously worked in Brooklyn. The Portland *Transcript,* in an article about the factory's opening, reported, "An experienced and skilful artist, who made a glass set costing $4,000, for Mrs. President Lincoln, is to have charge of the work."[131] Thirty years later an article in a Corning, New York, paper about Corning Glass Works said, "Before coming here, this company made for President Lincoln a set of tableware of flint glass and various colors and later on made a superb set for General Grant."[132] The reference to Grant's set is correct, but the reference to the Lincoln set is puzzling. Perhaps some of the blanks—the pieces of blown glass made for cutting—were produced in the Brooklyn Flint Glass Works before the company moved to Corning in 1868, becoming Corning Glass Works. Large orders of this kind were often shared by one or more companies. It is quite possible that both John Hoare, proprietor of the cutting shop within the Brooklyn company, and the blowing room of the Brooklyn Flint Glass Works assisted Dorflinger with this order.

The press charged Mrs. Lincoln with extravagance for some of her purchases, including the china, but the glass purchase occasioned no particular comment. As the Civil War raged, the Lincolns decided to abolish state dinners for reasons of

FIG. 27. *Compote from the set first ordered by the Lincolns in 1861.*
Brooklyn, New York: Greenpoint Glass Works of Christian Dorflinger, 1861,
or E. V. Haughwout & Company, 1866. Ht. 8¹/₄″.

economy. They continued, however, to have afternoon and evening receptions for the public with refreshments.[133] On February 5, 1862, Mrs. Lincoln held a ball, called by the press a "Presidential Party." One paper gushed:

> There has been a social innovation at the White House and the experiment has been a brill[i]ant success. Hitherto there have been but two variations in the social amenities of that establishment, namely State dinners and "receptions" the former dedicated to the entertainment principally of Foreign Ministers and heads of Departments, the latter to "the people"... every one high or low, gentle or ungentle, washed or unwashed who chooses to go.... Mrs. Lincoln hit upon the expedient of a Presidential Party... cards of invitation were issued to about 500 persons... and the result was a complete success.[134]

Another newspaper described the supper room as

> a coup d'oeil of dazzling splendor, fruits and flowers, and blazing lights, and sparkling crystal, and inviting confections were everywhere.... Upon the center of the principal table rose a magnificent vase, five feet high, filled with natural flowers, wreaths of which gracefully twined about the sides and base of the vase....[135]

The success of Mrs. Lincoln's party was overshadowed by the death a few weeks later of her son Willie. Official entertaining was curtailed for the next year. The two dozen cut goblets purchased through Webb and Beveridge, Washington retailers, in November 1864 and January 1865 were probably stock items meant for Lincoln family meals, for the cost was only $15 a dozen.[136] Despite reduced entertaining, both the glass and the china must have suffered considerable breakage. Early in 1865 Mrs. Lincoln ordered a set of china and more glassware, both from J. K. Kerr's Philadelphia establishment, China Hall. The porcelain was in a new pattern, with a buff-colored band around the rim and with no coat of arms. The glassware probably matched the earlier set, because no new serving pieces appear on the invoice, and the design is called "President's Pattern." The invoice lists

4 Dozen Goblets rich cut stem and Elegantly Engraved	@ $24.00 per doz.
4 Dozen Champagne glasses & Engraved	@ $20.00 [per doz.]
4 Dozen Claret glasses to match the above	@ $18.00 [per doz.]
4 Dozen Burgundy glasses rich cut stem and Engraved	@ $15.00 [per doz.]
4 Dozen Madeira glasses rich cut & Engraved Star President's Pattern	@ $21.50 [per doz.]
4 Dozen Sherry glasses rich cut and Engraved	@ $15.00 [per doz.]
4 Dozen Bohemian hock glasses ruby Engraved	@ $22.75 [per doz.]
4 Dozen Cordial glasses rich cut & Engraved	@ $15.00 [per doz.]
over 3 Champagne glasses	$ 5.00
2 Burgundy glasses	$ 2.50[137]

The total charge for the glassware was $612.50. Except for the Madeira and hock glasses, the prices and descriptions indicate that the pieces were engraved alike. Whether the Madeira glasses were more expensive because they had ruby bowls like the hocks, or because they were more elaborately engraved, is impossible to say. There are, however, two sizes of ruby-bowled glasses in the White House collection: a hock size and a smaller dessert-wine size (fig. 31).

It seems likely that Kerr's supplier was required to match the existing White House glassware. Although the patterns of some companies were protected by design registration, enforcement was difficult. Glass companies commonly advertised that they could cut and engrave glassware to match any existing pattern. The words "Engraved Star" on the invoice do not describe the Lincoln-pattern glassware very well, but "President's Pattern" does seem to indicate a reorder of an existing pattern. The only other stemware still in the White House from this period does not have engraved stars; if the Madeira glasses were engraved with stars in a different pattern, they have vanished.

Kerr's billhead advertised "French and English China and Glassware," but a letter in the White House files from William Dorflinger to Abby Gunn Baker identified the set as American. Dorflinger wrote, "The glassware indicated in the bill of January 30th, 1865, sold by J. R. Kerr of Philadelphia, was not made by us, but by the New England Glass Co., of Cambridge, Mass."[138] Wartime inflation had more than doubled the cost of fine glassware. The lower price for the 1865 order, compared with the 1861 order, must derive from the fact that the second order was smaller and did not include serving pieces. On March 25 Kerr billed "His Excellency Abraham Lincoln" $92 for "4 decanters rich cut glass."[139]

Before Lincoln's assassination in April 1865 the glass had been little used. The inventory of May 26, several days after Mrs. Lincoln had moved out, listed "1 Full Sett China with Finger Bowls Goblets & Champagne Glasses enough, All fine except Wine Decanters."[140] Obviously a cursory inventory, it does not mention the older glassware still in the house.

Andrew Johnson

It was summer before President Johnson and his family could move to the White House. They found the mansion in a shabby state, suffering from the hordes of petitioners who had assembled there daily during the war to await a word with the President. Souvenir hunters too had been permitted nearly free access to the lower floors of the White House while Mrs. Lincoln packed to leave. The house had been ransacked, losing many small items through petty theft. As one writer put it, "The rabble ranged through [the mansion] at will. Silver and dining ware were carried off and have never been recovered."[141]

Ill health kept Eliza Johnson from running the White House or attending social affairs. The Johnson's elder married daughter, Martha Patterson, acted as hostess. She took charge of the refurbishing that summer, winning much praise.

On July 10, 1865, B. B. French, the commissioner of public buildings and, as such, in charge of purchasing, wrote the following to E. V. Haughwout & Company:

> *In accordance with the wishes of the President, you will be pleased to examine thoroughly the silver at the President's House, the set of china known as the solferino service, with the U. S. coat of arms and replace such of the set of silver as has been broken, and also to furnish for the House a set of glass ware such as Mrs. Patterson may select, the whole expense not to exceed seven thousand dollars.*[142]

The following January Haughwout supplied a large set of china to match the remnants of the solferino set ordered by Mrs. Lincoln in 1861, some new and replated silver, and "one set of rich cut and engraved flint glassware with crest of U. S." Haughwout's total bill was $7,090; the glassware cost $2,596.[143] Included were

72 goblets	*48 Champagnes*
48 Clarets	*48 Hocks*
48 wines	*24 Cordials*
48 roman punch glasses	*12 quart decanters*
12 pint decanters	*6 Claret decanters*
48 [pint] caraffs	*6 sugars*
6 celery glasses	*4 Cake bowls*
8 side dishes	*48 finger bowls*
48 ice cream plates	

Judging from the shapes listed, Mrs. Patterson did *not* choose a new set, but reordered the pattern chosen in 1861 by Mrs. Lincoln. No individual prices are given, so it is impossible to compare the prices per item with the prices of the glass ordered the previous year from J. K. Kerr. No colored glasses are mentioned, although the hock glasses could have been green ones. Civil War inflation makes comparison difficult between this set and the $1,500 set ordered in 1861, but it is likely that they were similar in size. Although stemware was ordered several more times, this is the last order in this pattern to include serving pieces.

By comparing the numbers ordered by Mrs. Patterson with the numbers still in the White House, we can deduce which serving pieces might have been ordered in 1861. Four celery vases (fig. 30) in this pattern remain, probably all from this order, though they were a standard item in 1861. There are seven compotes (fig. 27) in the White House. Their sizes vary slightly, but such variations are characteristic of free-blown glassware of the period. Four are probably the cake bowls ordered in 1866, and three are from the earlier order, although there are no discernible differences in the engraving. Another is in the Metropolitan Museum of Art, so it seems that at least four were ordered each time. None of the remaining inventories show more than six sugar bowls. If the bowls were included in 1861, they had all been broken by 1866. Only one lid is left in the White House; the bowls are all missing (figs. 33, 34). The emblem engraved on the remaining sugar lid is slightly simpler than that on the majority of the remaining pieces, including neither banner nor motto. However, the compotes and celeries, some of which must be from this order, have the full insignia. None of the claret decanters from the listing remain. We cannot even be certain what the side dishes looked like, although one shallow bowl remains that might be one (fig. 30). The claret decanters were probably identical in shape to the quart and pint decanters (fig. 25), but with handles.

Exactly where the glass was produced is still in question. Haughwout's blanks came from the Brooklyn Flint Glass Works, which in 1864 had been sold by its founder, John L. Gilliland, to Amory Houghton. John Hoare was proprietor of the cutting shop attached to the glassworks, but he also had a second shop on Commercial Street adjacent to or in Dorflinger's Greenpoint factory. Dorflinger had moved in 1863 to White Mills, Pennsylvania, leaving his factory to be run by two associates, Bailey and Dobelman. He had not yet started the cutting shop in his White Mills factory. Whether the cutting was done in a shop maintained by Haughwout in an unknown location in Brooklyn, or by Hoare at one of his two locations, is impossible to

say; the latter seems more likely. The only contemporary description of Haughwout's facility is in a series of letters from Francis Nicol to Samuel Du Pont in 1860.
At that time Du Pont was the official host of a group of Japanese envoys—the same
visitors that James Buchanan's niece Harriet Lane had entertained with such
aplomb. Nicol, a partner in E. V. Haughwout & Company, had offered to escort the
Japanese to "our establishment" and show them the cutting of glass. He took them
to Brooklyn to see the manufacture of flint and colored glass.[144] Nicol must have
shown them the Brooklyn Flint Glass Works, and, from the letter, it seems that the
cutting may have been done on the premises.

With the creation of a new office, steward of the White House, and the appoint-
ment of William Slade to the position, an inventory was taken on February 28, 1867.
It listed exactly the quantity of glassware ordered from Haughwout, with a notation
that two champagnes, one hock, one wineglass, and one punch glass had arrived
broken. No mention was made of the older glassware, then probably in storage.[145]

President Johnson entertained frequently, so the tableware suffered much wear
and tear. Wine was served during dinners. Afterward, coffee was usually offered in
the Red Room, along with cordials, wine, and whiskey. The latter was now an after-
dinner drink, though not customarily served to women. Roman punch, made with
whiskey or rum and served in conical, handled punch glasses (fig. 25), was offered
between courses.[146] Martha Patterson presided at her father's dinners. According to
a description of her decorations for the last state dinner of Johnson's administration:

*The table was arranged for forty persons, each guest's name being upon the
plate designated on the invitation list. In the centre stood three magnificent*

73

Elder married daughter of President Andrew Johnson, Martha Patterson stood in as social hostess for her ailing mother, Eliza. The assassination of Lincoln in 1865 brought former Vice President Johnson and his family to the Executive Mansion. During his term the creation of the office of White House steward encouraged more complete inventories of the mansion's glass collection.

ANDREW JOHNSON NATIONAL HISTORIC
SITE, GREENEVILLE, TENNESSEE

ormolu [gilded bronze] ornaments, filled with fadeless French flowers, while, beside each plate, was a bouquet of odorous greenhouse exotics. It was not the color or design of the Sevres China, of green and gold, the fragile glass, nor yet the massive plate, which attracted my admiration, but the harmony of the whole, which satisfied and refreshed.[147]

On December 26, 1868, the White House purchased four dozen cheap "punch tumblers" from J. W. Boteler & Brothers, crockery and glass dealers in Washington, D. C., evidently for the customary New Year's reception. Six dozen more were rented a few days later. The preparations for the reception must have shown Mrs. Patterson the deficiencies in the glassware set, for on January 19, 1869, another large purchase of table glass was made from Boteler. That most items in this purchase were replacements is shown by the odd quantities of stemware. Some new types were also included. On the voucher are listed

8 Diamond Cut and Eng'd Goblets	@ $ 5.00 ea.
11 [Diamond Cut and Eng'd] Champagnes	$ 4.00 ea.
15 [Diamond Cut and Eng'd] Clarets	$ 3.75 ea.
5 [Diamond Cut and Eng'd] Hocks	$ 4.00 ea.
9 [Diamond Cut and Eng'd] Wines	$ 3.50 ea.
4 [Diamond Cut and Eng'd] Liqueurs	$ 3.50 ea.
14 [Diamond Cut and Eng'd] Punch Glasses	$ 4.50 ea.
3 [Diamond Cut and Eng'd] Ice Cream Plates	$ 3.50 ea.
5 [Diamond Cut and Eng'd] Finger Bowls	$ 5.00 ea.
1 [Diamond Cut and Eng'd] Decanter	$18.00
23 [Diamond Cut and Eng'd] Clarets	$ 2.50 ea.
6 [Diamond Cut and Eng'd] Ruby [Clarets]	$ 1.00 ea.
75 U. S. Engraved Crests	$ 1.50 ea.
40 Lava Champagnes	$ 1.50
27 Diamond Cut Green Hocks	$ 2.50
15 [Diamond Cut] and Eng. Clarets	$ .65
7 [Diamond Cut and Eng.] Spanish wines	$ .50
16 [Diamond Cut and Eng.] Cordials	$ .75
32 Lava Clarets	$ 1.50
24 [Lava] Wines	$ 1.00[148]

This is the only invoice on which the charge for engraving the U. S. crest (on 74 pieces of stemware and a decanter) is listed separately. All the items as far down as the decanter must have been replacements of the Lincoln-pattern service, but the manufacturer is unknown. Boteler was a retailer, like Kerr. He would have placed an order wherever he could have obtained the lowest prices.

Of the cheaper items, the lava champagnes, clarets, and wines might refer either to a pattern or to a color. A different quantity of each shape was ordered, suggesting that these are replacements, but there is no lava-colored glass in the White House today. The six ruby clarets probably matched the ones ordered earlier to go with the Jackson-pattern service. The 27 diamond-cut green hocks *might* have matched the Lincoln-pattern service, but the invoice shows no extra charge for an engraved crest. The clarets, Spanish wines, and cordials—all for less than a dollar each—do not seem to match anything. Purchased in such odd quantities, they must also have been replacements.

Ulysses S. Grant

When the Grants entered the White House in March 1869, they ordered its redecoration. Most of the work was completed during the summer, which they spent at the New Jersey shore. Upon their return, they purchased a coat-of-arms dinner service from Boteler.[149] A few odd pieces of glass were bought at the same time, but no immediate replacements of stemware were necessary.

Two inventories were taken on December 13 and 14, 1869—nine months after Grant assumed office. The December 13 inventory is handwritten, now in the National Archives. The one taken the following day exists both in handwritten and in printed form, for it was included in a report to Congress.[150] (Both inventories are given in full in Appendix I.) The glass totals on the two inventories differ widely; it appears that the first inventory was not completed, so a second was made. The first lists "Glass, New," "Glass, Old Set," and "Glass, Old." Under the first heading most of the 1866 purchase is listed. The inventory taken the following day is much more complete, but it groups both the Jackson-pattern and Lincoln-pattern sets together as "Coat of Arms glass." To compound the confusion, the handwritten second inventory is missing 14 entries that appear in the printed version.

Listed in the printed inventory are 52 bouquet holders (fig. 38)—conical bud vases that originally had silver stands. Many of the vases remain, but the stands have all been lost. Individual bouquets are mentioned in the description of Mrs. Patterson's last state dinner (pages 73–74), so apparently the bouquet holders had been purchased during the Johnson administration. The remaining ones are either colorless or red. They have an icelike surface of crushed glass, and gilding around the rim. The bouquet holders have no engraving, so they were probably relatively inexpensive. They are made of lead glass; thus, they are likely to be American or English. (Continental glass rarely contained lead, though a similar "ice" glass was made in Europe in a nonlead version.) The holders were used in the White House from the late 1860s until the end of the century. Although they do not appear on any existing invoices for glassware, they are on all the inventories after this one.

On November 17, 1870, the Grants bought from Boteler three dozen each of goblets, champagnes, and wineglasses for $145. At $16 a dozen, they must not have been an addition to the state service, although the notation "Cut and Eng. Grant pattern" appears on the invoice.[151] Late in 1870 the Corning newspaper told its readers: "The Corning Glass Works have received an order from President Grant for one thousand dollars worth of glassware."[152] It is difficult to identify the particular order. Corning Glass Works was having financial problems at the time; it may be that the order actually went to John Hoare, who maintained cutting shops in Brooklyn and on the second floor of the Corning Glass Works. It is not even clear whether the order was a private one for the Grants or a government order for the White House. The only invoice in government records for the period is the one mentioned above for $145. The invoice and the newspaper may refer to the same order, for newspapers frequently exaggerated the prices of such orders.

Julia Grant enjoyed her role as White House hostess, entertaining grandly. The couple served wine at smaller receptions and fruit punch at larger ones. Hard liquor had rarely been offered at the White House since Mrs. Polk's ban; wine was more common because most European guests expected it.

In January 1870 the Grants gave a state dinner for Prince Arthur of Britain. The food alone at the 29-course meal was said to have cost $1,500;[153] the several wines ran nearly as high. Such gargantuan meals took so *(Continued on page 80)*

TOP: FIG. 28. Cordial glass in the Lincoln pattern, 1865–85. Ht. 3 1/2".

BOTTOM: FIG. 29. The engraved insignia on the shallow bowl in figure 30. E. V. Haughwout, 1866. This design, without the motto, is on some cordial glasses, on the green hock glasses, on some ruby-bowled wineglasses, and on the sugar bowl lid.

LEFT: FIG. 30. *Finger bowl, ice cream plate, shallow bowl (perhaps called a "side dish"), and celery vase from the service first ordered by the Lincolns in 1861 and reordered through 1902. Ht. of vase 9 $^1/_4$".*

ABOVE: FIG. 31. *Goblet, champagne glass, and four wineglasses from the same set. Ht. of goblet 6 $^1/_2$".*

RIGHT: FIG. 32. *The engraved insignia on the ice cream plate in figure 30. This variant does not appear on any other pieces in this service. A sample plate given to The Corning Museum of Glass by Miss Isabel Dorflinger has the full insignia.*

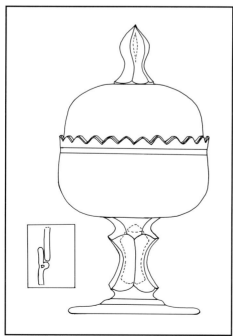

ABOVE: *FIG. 33. Sugar bowl lid from the Lincoln-pattern service. Brooklyn: probably E. V. Haughwout & Co., 1866. Ht. 4". No bowls remain in the White House.*

LEFT: *FIG. 34. Drawing of the lid in figure 33, showing the kind of sugar bowl base that would have matched it.*

RIGHT: *FIG. 35. Sherry glass from the Lincoln-pattern service, 1861–73. Ht. 4³/₄". This glass was removed from the White House in 1881 by President and Mrs. Rutherford B. Hayes.*

DRAWING BY DONNA MARMUSCAK
OPPOSITE: COLLECTION OF THE HAYES
PRESIDENTIAL CENTER, FREMONT, OHIO

(Continued from page 75) long to serve that after-dinner conversation became a nearly lost art. According to a contemporary account:

> *It is the evening of the President's state dinner. The guests are not only invited, but expected to be punctually in their places at seven o'clock P.M. President and Mrs. Grant are already in the Red Room, awaiting the company. . . . Mrs. Grant is in full evening dress—jewels, laces, and all the et ceteras to match. Her lady guests are attired as handsomely as herself, and the gentlemen are expected to wear black swallow-tail coats and white neckties. . . . In the beginning of the feast, fruits, flowers, and sweetmeats grace the table, whilst bread and butter only give a Spartan simplicity to the "first course" which is composed of a French vegetable soup . . . followed by a French croquet of meat. Four admirably trained servants remove the plates between each course, and their motions are as perfect as clockwork. . . . The "third" course of the dinner is composed of a filet of beef, flanked on each side by potatoes the size of a walnut, with plenty of mushrooms to keep them company. The next course is . . . made up entirely of the luscious legs of partridges . . . we pass on to the dessert, not omitting to say that the meridian or noon of the feast is marked by the guests being served bountifully with frozen punch. As a general rule, wine is served about every third course. Six wine glasses of different sizes, and a small bouquet of flowers are placed before each guest at the beginning. . . . The dessert is inaugurated by the destruction of a rice pudding. . . . After the rice pudding, canned peaches, pears and quinces are served. Then follow confectionery, nuts, ice-cream, coffee, and chocolate, and with these warm, soothing drinks the Presidential entertainment comes to an end, the host and his guests repair to the Red Room, and after fifteen minutes spent in conversation the actors in a state dinner rapidly disappear.[154]*

When preparations began at the White House for Nellie Grant's 1874 wedding, the Grants ordered more of their new state china service as well as additional pieces of Mrs. Lincoln's solferino porcelain service. They also ordered two types of glassware in the fall of 1873—a substantial reorder of the Lincoln-pattern service and a less expensive glassware set as well. All the glassware and china were ordered from Boteler, with the Lincoln-pattern glassware produced in John Hoare's cutting shop in Corning.

This order was first announced in the Corning paper on August 1, 1873: "Mr. John Hoare, of the glass cutting department of the Corning Glass Works, has received an order for several thousand dollars worth of glass ware for the State dinner service, at the White House."[155] In October the paper reported: ". . . the elegant glass ware (to supply the President's State Dinner Service) made at the Corning Glass Works, and cut and engraved in the Cutting Department, by Mr. Hoare, will be on exhibition at the Glass Works, during each day and evening, next Wednesday, Thursday, Friday."[156]

The extent of national curiosity about the furnishings of the presidential mansion is shown by an article in an Oakland, California, newspaper about the glassware. Under the heading "Republican Simplicity," the paper commented:

> *At the Corning Glass-Works, a set of glass . . . destined for the Presidential mansion has just been completed. It consists of two dozen goblets, which are*

cut about half way up the bowl, the remainder of the bowl being richly engraved, and prominent among it is the United States coat-of-arms; four dozen champagne glasses and saucer bowl, . . . two dozen regular champagne glasses . . . six dozen canary colored hock glasses; seven dozen ruby-bowl, flint-stem sauterne glasses. These colored glasses are very superior . . . three dozen punch glasses with handles; four dozen ice cream plates, cut and engraved as the glasses. The value of the glass is about $2000.[157]

Although the newspaper had the quantities of glassware wrong, its descriptions of the cutting and engraving and of the handled punch glasses are helpful. It is clear that the pieces matched the Lincoln-pattern service in use since 1861. The total price was $2,029.65, and the following quantities were delivered on November 24, 1873:

$3^2/_{12}$ doz. Cordials	@ $54.00 per doz.
3 doz. Ice Creams	67.00 per doz.
$6^5/_{12}$ doz. Sherries	45.00 [per doz.]
3 doz. Madeiras	45.00 [per doz.]
$1^{11}/_{12}$ doz. Goblets	72.00 [per doz.]
10/12 doz. Clarets	57.00 [per doz.]
$1^1/_{12}$ doz. Finger bowls	79.20 [per doz.]
$5^1/_{12}$ doz. Green Hocks	60.00 [per doz.]
$1^8/_{12}$ doz. Punch glasses	60.00 [per doz.]
$6^1/_{12}$ doz. Rose Sauternes	60.00 [per doz.]
$2^8/_{12}$ doz. Champagnes	72.00 [per doz.][158]

Bud vases and bonbon dishes filled with spring flowers brighten a state dinner given by President Ulysses S. Grant for the joint high commissioners of the United States and Great Britain. (The bud vases are shown in figure 38.) Pierce had added the bonbon dishes to Monroe's French plateau. Water carafes and wineglasses in the Lincoln pattern further embellish the table.

REPRODUCED FROM FRANK LESLIE'S ILLUSTRATED NEWSPAPER, APRIL 1, 1871

81

All the glasses are described as "cut and engraved," with no mention of seal or crest, although they must have been so engraved. The largest quantities ordered are of the red-bowled and green glasses, perhaps explaining why so many remain at the White House today. The order does not, contrary to the newspaper account, include two sizes of rose-colored glasses or two types of champagne glasses. The green and red glasses may not have been reordered as often as the colorless ones; they are specifically mentioned only in 1865 and 1868, before the 1873 order.

Curiously, the Grants purchased another set of cut glass at the same time from Boteler.[159] It was also described as "cut and engraved," but the prices were much lower than those of the set above. The second set was probably a stock pattern for family use, perhaps to accompany the plain rose-banded china that Mrs. Grant had purchased for the same purpose in 1870. The smaller service was delivered the day after the state service. It included five dozen claret glasses, six dozen Madeira and saucer champagne glasses, and four dozen sherry glasses, goblets, and cordials, at prices ranging from $9 a dozen for the sherries and cordials to $24 a dozen for the saucer champagnes. Since Hoare's shop was busy with the state service, Boteler likely sent this order to a different firm, possibly to Dorflinger's in White Mills, a firm known to have worked on several personal orders for the Grants.[160]

The White House collection has a number of glasses with cut stems, engraved with a meandering ivy vine, that may be the remains of this order. Goblets and two sizes of wineglasses (fig. 36) remain. Until the 1950s the collection also had a matching sherry glass. There are two less elegant red-stained glasses engraved to match (fig. 37). Made of nonlead glass, they must have been added later.

Nellie Grant's wedding to Englishman Algernon Sartoris, on the morning of May 21, was the social highlight of Grant's second term. Two hundred fifty guests found a White House filled with flowers. Following the ceremony in the East Room, the guests were served an elegant wedding breakfast at 11:30, where they sipped Roman punch—the iced whiskey or rum punch usually offered during state dinners.[161]

Nearly two years later, on January 4, 1876, another detailed inventory was taken.[162] The inventory is not much more helpful than previous ones, for it does not separate the "state set" from the rest of the glassware. There are 95 green claret glasses, as well as 104 green hock glasses; we can only hypothesize that one type is from the earlier Jackson-pattern set, and the other from the Lincoln-pattern set. (This inventory appears in full in Appendix II.)

Rutherford B. Hayes

Rutherford B. Hayes, inaugurated in March 1877, and his wife, Lucy, were determined to set a tone of respectability at the White House following political scandals that had plagued the Grant administration. Wealthy in his own right, Hayes did not find the expense of running the President's mansion as burdensome as had some previous Presidents. The presidential salary had doubled—from $25,000 to $50,000—beginning with Grant, and there was no need for extensive redecorating of the White House, which had been done in 1869.

"Miss Grundy" (actually the newspaperwoman Austine Snead), a society columnist for the *New York Daily Graphic* and for other papers, wrote frequently about White House social affairs during the Hayes years. To her we are indebted for information about the first large state dinner given by the Hayeses, on April 20, 1877, for the Russian Grand Duke Alexis. Six wineglasses, a water glass, and an individual bouquet holder stood at each place. The next week, Miss Grundy reported: "A lively topic of discussion has been opened here . . . whether or no Mrs. Hayes really means to banish wine from state dinners to natives in future."[163] For several weeks the newspapers were full of this topic. Although Mrs. Hayes did not drink at all, her husband had no objection to wine. Soon after this dinner, however, President Hayes made the decision that no alcohol would be served in the White House, except at state dinners in honor of distinguished foreigners. "It seemed to me," he said, "that to exclude liquors from the White House would be wise and useful as an example, and would be approved by good people generally."[164] Although newspapers credited Mrs. Hayes with the change, the decision was, in fact, made by her husband. It was not until after she left the White House that the nickname "Lemonade Lucy" was bestowed upon her by journalists.

President and Mrs. Hayes did serve a Roman punch between courses at a number of their dinners, and "Punch au Kirsch" is listed on one of their menus.[165] At least one newspaperman insisted that the Roman punch contained rum, and that the waiters were careful to serve it abundantly to the guests they knew would prefer it.[166] However, President Hayes said that no rum—only rum flavoring—was used in the punch.[167] The cost of rum would certainly have shown up on the White House accounts if the steward had tried to serve it without presidential permission, so it would seem unlikely that the steward spiked the punch.

The Hayeses usually invited three dozen guests to their dinners. Even with the Grant's china purchases, the couple needed a new dinner set. Mrs. Hayes chose a service made by Haviland in France, with designs of American flora and fauna supplied by American artist Theodore Davis.[168] The initial installment of the service arrived in June 1880. Mrs. Hayes used it first at a banquet for President-elect James Garfield in November of that year.

The glass service was rarely used by the Hayes family, and there was little need to reorder it. Coffee, tea, and chocolate were the beverages served most often at receptions.[169] A surviving photograph of the table set for a luncheon given by Mrs. Hayes (page 87) shows the Lincoln-pattern water goblets and carafes on the table, along with the individual bouquet holders in silver stands, both of the large compotes from the Jackson-pattern service, and several diamond-pattern compotes holding fruit arrangements. One of the diamond-pattern compotes (fig. 39) remains in the White House.

A few orders for miscellaneous glassware were placed during Hayes's term. Three dozen cut tumblers were bought in March 1877; two dozen cut and engraved goblets were purchased in June of that year, and six dozen more goblets in April 1878. In March 1879 miscellaneous glassware was bought for $104; two cut-glass pitchers were purchased the following May, a dozen cut goblets in July 1880, and two dozen cut butter plates that November.[170] Presumably, the goblets and tumblers were all for water.

Perhaps inspired by the recent Centennial of the United States, President and Mrs. Hayes viewed the house and its furnishings as documents of history. Mrs. Hayes planned a collection of White House glassware and china and gathered several out-of-date pieces together in a group. She did not complete the collection before her husband's term expired. The glassware was moved to Fremont, Ohio, when she returned there in 1881.[171] With the Hayeses' support of temperance, it is ironic that the collection, now on view at the Hayes Presidential Center, in Fremont, consists mainly of drinking glasses and decanters. Among these are two shapes from the Lincoln-pattern service that are no longer in the White House collection: small cordial glasses (fig. 28) and conical sherry glasses (fig. 35).

James A. Garfield and Chester A. Arthur

President Hayes did not seek a second term; he was succeeded by his friend James A. Garfield, also from Ohio. Garfield probably intended to rescind the Hayes temperance rule, but in July, barely into his term of office, he was fatally shot by a disappointed office-seeker. During his brief Presidency he gave no state dinners. In June Colonel Rockwell, the White House purchasing agent, had ordered 12 dozen cut-glass goblets at $12 a dozen and nine cut-glass "comports" for $20 each.[172] At that price the goblets were certainly not engraved to match the Lincoln-pattern service, although they may have matched the ones ordered by Hayes at the same price.

Vice President Chester A. Arthur, a New York machine politician, became President upon Garfield's death. He found the Executive Mansion, which had not been redecorated since Grant's first term, to be in need of extensive work. Congress had voted Garfield $30,000 for repairs to the house, and Arthur spent it. He refused to move in until the first phase of the work was completed in early December. Eventually, he spent $110,000 on the most elaborate program of redecoration since 1814. In preparation, he sent 24 wagonloads of furnishings to a mammoth sale in April 1882.[173] Thirty barrels of china and glass were included in this sale.[174] An inventory taken the following month lists the glassware that remained. It is titled "List of Articles, in serviceable condition."[175] Under the heading "Crystal for State Dining Room" are the following:

89 Finger Glasses	78 Water Carafes
38 [Finger Glasses] Old Pattern	66 Ice Cream Saucers
46 [Finger Glasses] Plates	49 Liqueur & Brandy Glasses
91 Champagne Glasses	47 Roman Punch Glasses
278 Wine Glasses	45 Sherry Glasses
44 Goblets	49 Sauterne Glasses
157 Claret Glasses	16 Celery Glasses
11 Water Jugs	12 Crystal Stands
169 Hock Glasses (Green)	108 Hock Glasses (Pink)
16 Salt Cellars (for Silver Stands)	36 Bouquet Glasses for Holders
54 Decanters, Liqueur Bottles	
& Crystal Claret Jugs	

OPPOSITE: FIG. 36. Wineglasses, probably from a set ordered by the Grants in 1873. United States, 1865–75. Ht. of tallest 5 1/2".

ABOVE: FIG. 37. Ruby-stained and engraved wineglass matching the set in figure 36. Ht. 4 11/16".

BELOW: Lucy Hayes

Given Arthur's apparent disdain for old-fashioned furnishings, it is surprising that he left any of the glass from previous years in the pantry. Shortly after the sale Arthur, who was a widower, moved with his children into the presidential summer home on the grounds of the Soldiers' Home. At the same time Louis C. Tiffany and Associated Artists redecorated the state rooms of the White House in the newly popular "aesthetic" style. Silver, china, and a few pieces of miscellaneous glassware were bought from Tiffany & Company, the New York jewelry store, during the redecoration. Among the pieces were two "Flower Globes" for $15 each and one for $20,[176] all probably cut glass. Such globes—nearly spherical bowls—were commonly called rose bowls. The White House collection has three rose bowls (fig. 40), probably the Tiffany globes, although the lack of inventories in the 1880s and 1890s means that the bowls can be traced back only to 1901.

Arthur and his children returned to a White House ready for the formal entertaining the President enjoyed. Because his daughter was only 11, Arthur's sister, Mary McElroy, acted as his hostess. The genial President gave receptions and dinners as grand as those of the Hayeses. "I dined at the President's," wrote one guest.

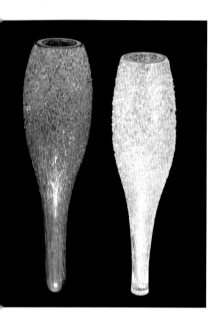

FIG. 38. *Ruby and colorless bud vases, gilded around rim. England or the United States, ca. 1865–69. Ht. of taller 6". Andrew Johnson's daughter, Martha, probably purchased the vases. An image from a stereopticon card (opposite) records the flower-filled vases in silver stands. (None of the stands remain in the White House.) The table is prepared for a luncheon given in 1881 by Mrs. Hayes. A Lincoln-pattern water goblet and a carafe accompany each place setting. Bowls ordered by Pierce and several compotes brim with fruit. On the sideboard, finger bowls await service.*

"The dinner was extremely elegant . . . the flowers, the damasks, the silver, the attendants, all showing the latest style and an abandon in expense and taste."[177]

The President's first state dinner, given for former President Grant and his wife, was elegant indeed. According to one account:

> *There were thirty-four plates on the long table, in the centre of which was a plateau mirror, on which were roses and lilies of the valley. . . . Around this elaborate centre decoration were ranged crystal compotes and cut-glass decanters. Large flat corsage bouquets of roses, tied with satin ribbons, were laid at each lady's plate, and small boutonnieres of rosebuds were provided for the gentlemen. The cards were of heavy gild-edged board, embossed with the national coat-of-arms in gold, below which the name of each guest was written. . . . Dinner was served in fourteen courses, with which there were served eight varieties of wines, each variety having an appropriate wine glass. The guests were two hours at the table. . . .[178]*

Arthur enlarged the seating capacity of the State Dining Room from 40 to 65 and expanded the musical entertainment offered after dinner. The President liked Mrs. Hayes's new dinner service, and he displayed much of it in the family dining room. Although he purchased silver serving pieces from Tiffany, he was apparently content with the existing glassware. He made no major glassware purchases, but he did rent glass from Boteler in the spring of 1884 and did buy seven dozen goblets and wineglasses from the firm in November.[179] At nearly $50 a dozen, they were probably additions to the Lincoln-pattern glassware. That fall Boteler also supplied six dozen cut and engraved goblets for $18 a dozen.[180] These may have matched the simple set ordered by the Grants, or they may have been of an entirely new pattern.

Grover Cleveland

Grover Cleveland, the nation's second bachelor President, took office on March 4, 1885. His sister Rose Cleveland acted as his hostess for the first 18 months of his term. During the summer of 1885 more glassware for the State Dining Room was purchased. Col. John W. Wilson, commissioner of public buildings, wrote M. W. Beveridge, a Washington retailer, for the names of glass manufacturers who could provide replacements for the White House state service. He received this reply:

> *July 28, 1885*
>
> *Col. Wilson*
>   *Below please find address of Glass Manufacturers as requested. Should you require any Table ware for White House I should be please to furnish it from any of the factories as low as you can get it from them.*
>
>   *Yours very truly,*
>   *M. W. Beveridge.*
>
> *C. Dorflinger & Sons. White Mills, Wayne Co. Pa*
> *Boston & Sandwich Glass Co. Boston, Mass.*
> *New England Glass Works, East-Cambridge, Boston, Mass.*
> *Mt. Washington Glass Works, New Bedford, Mass.*
> *Corning Glass Works, Corning, N.Y.[181]*

FIG. 39. Compote, probably ordered by Mrs. Grant or by Mrs. Hayes in the 1870s. United States, 1865–80. Ht. 7". The diamond-cutting comes so near the scalloped rim of this compote that the piece may have been cut down from a slightly taller original in an effort to erase chips. At least six compotes of this type as well as two Jackson-pattern compotes (then more than 50 years old) can be seen in the photograph on page 87.

The day before Beveridge's reply arrived, Wilson had received this proposal from Thomas G. Hawkes, a Corning glass cutter who was in Washington at the time:

I will furnish the following Glassware . . . equal in every prospect in quality of glass workmanship etc to samples, for the following prices.

4 Dz Finger Bowls to sample	*$25.00 Dz. 100.*
3 [Dz] Champs [to sample]	*23.[00 Dz.] 69.*
4 [Dz] Clarets [to sample]	*21.[00 Dz.] 84.*
4 [Dz] Goblets [to sample]	*25.[00 Dz.] 100.*
4 [Dz] Roman Punch Glasses [to sample]	*25.[00 Dz.] 100.*
4 [Dz] Brandies [to sample]	*18.[00 Dz.] 72.*
3 [Dz] Rine Wines [to sample]	*23.[00 Dz.] 69.*
6 [Dz] Madeiras [to sample]	*23.[00 Dz.] 138.*
4 [Dz] S. Sherries [to sample]	*18.[00 Dz.] 72.*
3 [Dz] White Wines [to sample]	*22.[00 Dz.] 66.*
2 [Dz] Burgundies [to sample]	*21.[00 Dz.] 42.*
6 [Dz] Ice Cream plates [to sample]	*23.[00 Dz.] 138.*
	$1050.

Very Resptf. Yours,
T. G. Hawkes
Rich Cut Glass Manufacturer, Corning, New York

References: Davis Collamore & Co., N.Y.   Gorham Mnfg. Co.   New York
J. E. Caldwell & Co.   Phila.   Richard Briggs   Boston[182]

Hawkes had only been in business for himself for five years, but he had been superintendent of John Hoare's cutting shop in 1873 when the last large order for White House glass arrived. Perhaps in Washington only by chance, Hawkes heard that the White House was about to purchase new glassware and acted swiftly to obtain the prestigious order. The prices seem unnaturally low; it is likely that Hawkes supplied the set at cost—possibly below cost—to secure the order.

By the time he received Beveridge's letter, Colonel Wilson had already decided to buy the glass from Hawkes, although the order was much smaller than Hawkes had proposed.

July 29, 1885

Thomas G. Hawkes

Sir:

> *Please deliver at the Executive Mansion in this City the following cut glass to be made in the best manner and similar to samples to be furnished you by the Steward at the Mansion.*

> *3 doz. finger bowls*
> *2 doz. Champagnes*
> *3 Doz. Clarets*
> *3 [Doz.] Goblets*
> *3 [Doz.] Roman Punches*
> *5 [Doz.] Madeiras (Red)*
> *3 [Doz.] Sherries*
> *1 [Doz.] White Wine (Red)*
> *5 [Doz.] ice cream plates*

> *The glass should be delivered as soon as convenient and certainly by October 1.*

> *Very Respectfully,*
> *John M. Wilson[183]*

Because Colonel Wilson ordered less glassware than Hawkes had suggested, the order came to only $640 and was delivered in October. This was an important commission for Hawkes, who was not slow to publicize it. An article appeared in the *New York Sun* when the glass was delivered and was copied in a trade paper and in the local Corning paper:

> *EXECUTIVE CUT GLASS*
>
> *A GLASS Company at Corning is now manufacturing a set of table glassware for the White House. The fifty dozen pieces ordered include for the most part what is called stem ware, i.e. goblets, tumblers, decanters, liqueurs, lemonades, etc. The light glasses are for the most part gold, ruby or amber ware. The order also includes Roman punch glasses, finger bowls, individual butters, ice cream plates, ice cream trays, caraffes, pitchers, and flagons. No pains have been spared to make each piece as perfect as possible. The slightest flaw that only a trained eye can see dooms the most valuable piece, so that its only use thereafter is as broken glass to be remelted. Of the 100 men in the shop only twenty of the best ones are employed on this order. The design engraved . . . consists of the American eagle perched on a shield above the*

FIG. 40. Cut-glass rose bowl, probably ordered by President Chester A. Arthur. United States, ca. 1882. Ht. 6³/₄″. This is one of three such bowls in the White House collection. It seems to be the earliest, probably purchased from Tiffany in 1882.

words "E Pluribus Unum." It is the design that has always ornamented ware for the White House. . . . The glass works in question removed to Corning from Brooklyn in 1868. In President Grant's administration the former shop supplied the White House with glassware. This establishment is now busy on the order for President Cleveland. All the work for both shops is turned out in the rough by the glass factory. . . . The work for the White House in the blowing room was done entirely by hand, no molds being used. There was included in it some gold-ruby ware, which requires unusual skill in manufacture. . . . The patterns on the glassware consist of sets of parallel lines, crossing at different angles, and forming many-sided diamonds and stars which are changed by additional complex cuts.[184]

This story, like the one in the Oakland paper in 1873, is full of inaccuracies. The pattern description is too general to allow much identification, but the evidence establishes that the glassware ordered was of the Lincoln pattern, not of the later Russian pattern. The engraved design as described matches that of the Lincoln pattern. The inclusion of both colored glasses and Roman punch glasses points to the Lincoln pattern, too, for the Russian service had neither. That Hawkes was directed to furnish glass identical to examples supplied him by the White House confirms that this was one more reorder of the Lincoln-pattern glass, rather than a completely new pattern. The Russian pattern, in fact, was not used at the White House until 1891.

There has been some confusion about this point. When Dorothy Daniel published her pioneering work, *Cut and Engraved Glass*, in 1950, she drew on an interview with Samuel Hawkes, son of Thomas G. Hawkes, to state that the Russian pattern was ordered for the White House in 1885.[185] Subsequent authors, including the present writer, have followed suit, thus corroborating her incorrect conclusion. The evidence actually proves Samuel Hawkes's memory wrong.

A contemporary description of Cleveland's first state dinner in 1886 mentions the glassware used at the table:

Interspersed the length of the board were glass and silver stands of conserves, bonbons, and salted almonds. . . . At each plate were set six Bohemian wine glasses, a cut-glass carafe, tumbler and champagne glass, Salt-cellars of cut glass, with golden shovels and silver pepper stands, were beside these.[186]

The stemware and individual carafes must have been the Lincoln-pattern glass, despite the label "Bohemian." By 1885 the pattern had been in use 24 years, and it was somewhat out of date. Although fashion had swung back toward heavier glass with more complex cutting, it was undoubtedly more economical to reorder the existing set than to choose a new one, an economy that might account for the continued use of the Lincoln pattern.

The service was ordered in quantity at least seven times—first by Mrs. Lincoln in 1861 and then in 1865, by Andrew Johnson's daughter in 1866 and 1869, by Mrs. Grant in 1873 (and possibly in 1870), by Grover Cleveland in 1885, and by Mrs. Theodore Roosevelt in 1902. In the White House collection are examples of a number of serving pieces, a finger bowl, a small bowl that might be one of the "side dishes" ordered in 1866, and an ice cream plate (fig. 30); goblets, saucer champagnes, two sizes of colorless wineglasses, green hock glasses, and red-bowled claret and sauterne glasses (fig. 31); and a punch glass. These pieces are undoubtedly a mixture of several orders supplied by Christian Dorflinger in 1861 and 1902, the New

England Glass Company in 1865, E. V. Haughwout or Hoare & Dailey in 1866, Hoare & Dailey in 1873, and Hawkes in 1885. It is likely that examples from all these orders remain in the White House.

There are minor differences in the engraved pattern on a number of pieces, but they are not consistent enough to enable identification by order. The differences in the engraving of the insignia are a little more apparent. None of the green hock glasses have the full insignia. Of the red glasses, some do and some do not. A sample ice cream plate that descended in the Dorflinger family (now in The Corning Museum of Glass) has the full insignia; the one at the White House is quite different, lacking the engraved pattern and the cartouche around the emblem (fig. 32). It is also quite flat, while the Dorflinger family plate has a deep depression in the center. The small "side dish," the sugar bowl lid, and the green glasses are alike in not having the motto or the shield on which the eagle perches. The cordial glasses at the Hayes Center and the one at the Everhart Museum, in Scranton, Pennsylvania (a Dorflinger family piece), have the full insignia, but at least one in a private collection does not.

A letter from William Dorflinger to Abby Gunn Baker in 1914 states that the glasses supplied by Dorflinger had the full insignia, but it also says that the New England Glass Company made the green glasses and the red glasses with modified insignia.[187] This cannot be entirely correct, since no green glasses were included in Kerr's invoice in 1865. It is obvious from the number of glasses ordered and the number left that most of the other orders must also have included glasses with the full insignia. Perhaps only the 1866 order from Haughwout had the variant engraving, for

Beneath a shaft of pulleys, glass cutters pose in the cutting shop of J. Hoare & Company in Corning about 1890. The shop was on the second floor of the Corning Glass Works. Hoare's skilled workmen had cut and engraved President Grant's 1873 purchase of glassware, produced in the Lincoln pattern.

91

FRANK LESLIE'S
ILLUSTRATED
NEWSPAPER

Entered according to Act of Congress, in the year 1886, by Mrs. FRANK LESLIE, in the Office of the Librarian of Congress at Washington.—Entered at the Post Office, New York, N. Y., as Second-class Matter.

No. 1,603.—Vol. LXII.]   NEW YORK—FOR THE WEEK ENDING JUNE 12, 1886.   [Price, 10 Cents. $4.00 Yearly.
13 Weeks, $1.00.

WASHINGTON, D. C.—THE WEDDING AT THE WHITE HOUSE, JUNE 2ND—THE MOTHER'S KISS.

FROM A SKETCH BY C. BUNNELL.—SEE PAGE 261.

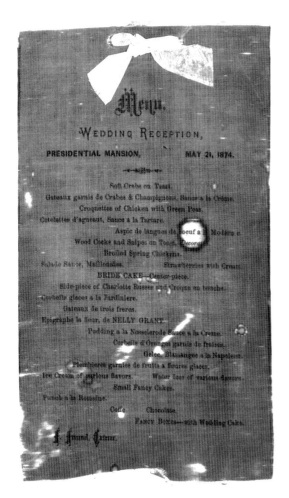

FAR LEFT: Bride of the first President to be married in the White House, Frances Folsom kisses her mother as Grover Cleveland accepts a congratulatory handshake. Twenty-one-year-old Frances lacked experience as a household manager. Nevertheless, she used the White House glassware frequently, proving to be one of the most popular women ever to serve as White House hostess.
LIBRARY OF CONGRESS

LEFT: Appetizing fare fit for a queen fills the wedding breakfast menu of Nellie Grant. The only daughter of President and Julia Grant, she wed an Englishman in 1874. Amid a flourish of flowers and fashions, the marriage ceremony took place in the East Room of the White House and became the crowning event of the Grants' social calendar. For the occasion, the happy parents ordered more of their new state service china and additional Lincoln-pattern glassware.
WHITE HOUSE

it was the one to include the side dishes and sugar bowls. But the compotes and celery vases from that order have the standard engraving, and the ice cream plate is yet another variation. Testing under longwave and shortwave ultraviolet lights revealed a number of color differences, none consistent with the engraving differences. Examples of the Lincoln-pattern set are in several private and museum collections. These pieces probably left the White House through President Arthur's sale in 1882 or, perhaps, through other sales. Without more documentation it is impossible to make positive attributions of most of them.

President Cleveland married 21-year-old Frances Folsom, the daughter of his law partner, in June 1886. The glamorous wedding and the youth and beauty of the bride created a national stir. Although the new Mrs. Cleveland—27 years her husband's junior—had never before managed a household, she proved to be a skilled hostess, entertaining at musicales, informal teas, and Saturday afternoon receptions for the public as well as at state dinners and receptions. When Cleveland lost the election of 1888 to Benjamin Harrison, Frances Cleveland is supposed to have startled the White House staff by informing them as she departed that she would be back in four years. Her prediction came true.[188]

*Between courses,
guests savor
the pleasure of
a state dinner,
held on
January 19,
1888, during the
administration
of Grover
Cleveland.
The President
entertained
the diplomatic
corps at the affair.*

REPRODUCED FROM *HARPERS WEEKLY*, FEBRUARY 4, 1888, WHITE HOUSE COLLECTION

The Russian Pattern

The Russian pattern in cut glass was designed in 1882 by Philip McDonald, a cutter for Hawkes, in Corning. The design was patented by McDonald and assigned to Hawkes, but that did not stop other companies from making it. The pattern appears in catalogs of the New England Glass Company and of John Hoare during the 1880s and 1890s. By 1900 it was an industry standard, in the repertoire of every glass cutting firm. McDonald did not name the design in his patent application, but by June 1885, the pattern was known by the name Russian. That month Richard Briggs, Hawkes's Boston agent, transmitted an order for "a large service of glass in the Russian pattern" from the newly appointed American minister to St. Petersburg.[189] According to Samuel Hawkes, son of Thomas G. Hawkes and later head of the firm, the pattern received its name because Count Bibesco, the Russian ambassador to the United States, ordered a service for the embassy in Washington, D. C.[190] That story has not been verified, however, and it seems more likely that the Russian minister would have preferred to show off glass made in Russia.

The glass blank for the Russian pattern was much thicker and heavier than that used for the Lincoln-pattern service, and the pattern is a complex one with deeply cut motifs. This "rich-cut" or "brilliant" style was just coming into vogue in the 1880s, and the Russian pattern was the first of that style to vary from motifs based on the standard diamonds and hobnails. It was first ordered for the White House in 1891 and reordered through 1918.

Polished and gleaming, tableware stands ready for service at a White House state dinner arranged in 1899 by President William McKinley for Spanish-American War hero Adm. George Dewey. Colored Lincoln-pattern wineglasses mingle with stemware displaying a new look for that day, the star-cut Russian pattern.

Benjamin Harrison

Benjamin Harrison, the grandson of President William Henry Harrison, took office in March 1889. Two months later Colonel Wilson, commissioner of public buildings, received a letter from T. G. Hawkes soliciting another glassware order. He replied:

> *I regret to say that it is not the custom to refurnish the Executive Mansion once in four years. Unfortunately Congress makes no appropriation for such elaborate expenditures, and for the coming year the funds available will hardly be sufficient to keep the Mansion in good order.[191]*

By 1891 additional funds were forthcoming, and Caroline Harrison ordered new plates, cups, and saucers. A skilled china painter, Mrs. Harrison conceived the design of the set. Each plate had an eagle in the center and was bordered with corn and goldenrod, plants native to North America. The china was ordered through M. W. Beveridge, the Washington retailer. At the same time Beveridge was invited to furnish the Executive Mansion with a new set of glassware. For the first time since 1861 a new design for the state glassware service was chosen. A letter to Beveridge from Col. Oswald Ernst, the new commissioner, revealed:

> *The samples of table glass which were submitted by you have been examined, and the one selected for acceptance has the straight shape and the Russian cut, with the coat of arms of the United States engraved in medallion, like the finished goblet.*[192]

The glassware was delivered in November, only a few months after the order had been placed (figs. 42, 43). Beveridge had the glass made by C. Dorflinger & Sons, the Pennsylvania company. Presumably the firm was responsible for the design of the insignia. Because Dorflinger did not employ enough copper-wheel engravers at the time, the seal on many of the glasses was engraved by Joseph Haselbauer. A Bohemian-born craftsman, Haselbauer worked in Corning for T. G. Hawkes, but he also did free-lance engraving for Dorflinger in his home workshop and in White Mills.[193] The engraving on each piece has the American eagle facing its left shoulder, toward the arrows in its talon (fig. 41). This is the reverse of the eagle on the Great Seal and of the one on the Harrison china.

In the letter to Beveridge, Ernst ordered the following quantities:

5 dozen goblets	*@ $46.50 per dozen*
5 [dozen] saucer champagne glasses	*45.50 [per dozen]*
5 [dozen] claret [glasses]	*43.00 [per dozen]*
5 [dozen] sauterne (wht.) [glasses]	*40.50 [per dozen]*
5 [dozen] sherry [glasses]	*40.50 [per dozen]*
5 [dozen] Apollinaris tumblers	*40.50 [per dozen]*
5 [dozen] Finger bowls	*46.50 [per dozen]*
5 [dozen] Ice Cream plates	*56.50 [per dozen]*
8 Water bottles	*10.00*
8 Decanters (1 qt.)	*12.00*

Although the usual five dozen place settings were ordered, the number of glasses per person was smaller than in the previous set, and there were only two serving pieces. The water bottles held as much as the decanters and were obviously meant to serve more than one person. Glass serving pieces, such as celery dishes, compotes, and sugar bowls ordered for previous sets, were never used in the White House with this glass; silver serving pieces had replaced them. Although the Russian-pattern service was reordered several times, this is the only order for decanters that has been located. Only five of them are left. Among the remaining odd stoppers is a very large one that appears to have been made for a two-quart decanter. It is thus possible that at one time the set included at least one extra-large decanter.

The sauterne glasses have the designation "wht," which means colorless in this context. Glass factory catalogs of this period show claret, hock, and wine as the three sizes available, with no mention of sauterne. Hock glasses were available in red, blue, green, and amber from many companies; they were the same size as the glasses designated as sauterne by Ernst. Usually the color came from a casing over colorless glass. The pattern was cut through the colored layer to provide a contrasting colorless background. Sometimes, however, the glass was entirely colored. The Harrisons may have preferred colorless glass, or they may not have wished to pay extra for the color. For whatever reason, colored glass in the Russian pattern was never used in the White House. Photographs of White House dinners around the turn of the century show the colored glasses from the previous service on the table with the Russian-pattern glass (pages 96, 104).

The Harrison glassware set cost $1,973.50. When the glass was paid for, procedure dictated that the voucher be stamped "Procured in open market at lowest market rate, the public exigencies requiring immediate delivery of the articles and performance of the work."[194]

The new glassware was mentioned in several books. Said one account:

> *The new set of cut-glass was made at White Mills, Pennsylvania. . . . It consists of five hundred and twenty separate pieces, and was specially ordered by the Government for the White House. On each piece of the set, from the mammoth centerpiece and punch-bowl to the tiny salt-cellars, is engraved the coat of arms of the United States. The execution of the order occupied several months, and cost $6,000.*[195]

There are obviously inaccuracies in the description above. Neither punch bowls nor saltcellars were included in the order, which totaled less than $2,000—but the glassware *was* made at White Mills. Another contemporary publication says:

> *Guests at the state dinners next winter will have the pleasure of eating off the new set of china which is now being manufactured. . . . In addition to the new china a full service of cut glass ware will also come from across the sea to go with it on state occasions. A variety of new patterns were submitted to the President and Mrs. Harrison's inspection a month or two ago, and they selected many novel and beautiful shapes. In the new collection there will be water goblets, claret, champagne and brandy glasses. The shield and eagle is cut deeply in each one.*[196]

This reporter was more accurate, except in her description of the glassware as European. None of the state services of glassware was ever imported.

Grover Cleveland (Second Term)

In the spring of 1893 with Grover Cleveland's reelection, the Clevelands returned to the White House. The First Lady, finding Mrs. Harrison's new china and glass in use, decided to purchase additional items. In June 1894 "6 Cut glass Flagons with silver tops" (fig. 45) were bought from Boteler for $25.[197] That fall the White House bought from the same source five dozen cut punch glasses at $15 a dozen and six cut water bottles for $12 apiece.[198] At this price the water bottles were probably replacements for the Russian set. The punch glasses must have been cut more simply, probably in the strawberry-diamond and fan pattern, because later White House orders specify that pattern for punch glasses. Made by every cutting shop, the design was directly related to the diamond motifs first popular in the 1790s.

At his lathe, Joseph Haselbauer, a Bohemian-born craftsman, engraves a decanter at T. G. Hawkes & Company in Corning, New York. Haselbauer engraved the Presidential Seal on many White House orders between 1866 and 1910, working on both the Lincoln-pattern and the Russian-pattern sets.

By 1896 when the Clevelands were finishing their second term, the Russian-pattern set needed further replacements. Commissioner Wilson wrote to Beveridge:

> *I requested the steward of the Executive Mansion to visit your establishment and obtain the prices of certain glass required to replace broken pieces from a set furnished by you in 1891. He brought me the reply . . . and I find the difference between prices paid in 1891 and those at present to be considerable. . . . It has occurred to me that possibly there might have been some misunderstanding . . . whether the figures submitted . . . are for the same style exactly as furnished by you in 1891.[199]*

The new prices that shocked Wilson reflected about a 20 percent increase over five years. On April 29 Wilson wrote again, this time confirming a lesser increase, one that was about half of that suggested originally. He added, "It is understood that those prices cover engraving and delivery. Samples can be obtained from the White House Steward."[200] According to a brochure advertising T. G. Hawkes and Company, published about 1897, Beveridge placed this order with Hawkes.[201] The following glassware was delivered in July:

1½ Doz. cut goblets with U. S. crest	*@ $51.00 a doz.*
1 [Doz. cut] saucer champagnes	
[with U. S. crest]	*50.00 [a doz.]*
1 [Doz. cut] claret glasses [with U. S. crest]	*47.30 [a doz.]*
1½ [Doz. cut] sherry	
[glasses with U. S. crest]	*44.50 [a doz.]*
1 [Doz. cut] champagne tumblers	
[with U. S. crest]	*44.50 [a doz.]*
1 [Doz. cut] finger bowls [with U. S. crest]	*51.00 [a doz.]*

1 [Doz. cut finger bowl] plates
        [with U. S. crest]   *62.00 [a doz.]*
2 [Doz. cut] handled punch cups,   *12.50 [a doz.]*
        Strawberry-diamond & Fan[202]

Why Beveridge gave this order to T. G. Hawkes instead of to Dorflinger is unknown. It is probable that the Hawkes firm, then smaller than the Dorflinger company, was willing to do the work at a lower price for the prestige. Hawkes was using Dorflinger stemware blanks in the 1890s, although the blanks he used for larger pieces were made by Corning Glass Works.

A comparison of the shapes ordered in 1891 and the replacements ordered in 1896 shows that the size formerly called sauterne glasses became wineglasses, and the Apollinaris tumblers came to be called champagne tumblers. A contemporary Hawkes catalog shows six sizes of tumblers; the Apollinaris tumblers are taller than champagne tumblers. The ones left in the White House are all in the smaller champagne size, although they might well have been used for Apollinaris, an English mineral water popular around the turn of the century. This is the only order in which the plates are referred to as finger bowl plates instead of ice cream plates.

William McKinley

The Clevelands left the White House for the second time with the inauguration of William McKinley in 1897. Mrs. McKinley was an invalid who took little part in the social life of the administration. Access to McKinley's receptions was more restricted than it had been to Cleveland's, but the White House was still crowded on those occasions. That year Colonel Bingham chastised Beveridge by letter:

> It has just been observed that one of the Vases sold by you to this office . . . has been cracked and rivetted. I am therefore unwilling to pay more than half price for the vase. . . . I will add that you ought to be ashamed to deliver goods in such condition to the Executive Mansion.[203]

Mrs. McKinley ordered replacements for the Russian-pattern glassware in the summer of 1898; once more they were provided by Hawkes, although ordered from Beveridge. The Corning paper reported, "T. G. Hawkes & Co. are making a service of cut glass for the White House, it being the third order from the Government this concern has had since the Works were established here in 1880."[204] The prices were the same as those in the previous order. Hawkes supplied

2 dozen goblets	*1 [dozen] ice cream plates*
2 [dozen] claret glasses	*1 [dozen] salt cellars*
1 [dozen] wine glasses	*1 [dozen] water bottles*
2 [dozen] champagne saucers	*1 dozen Punch Glasses*
1¹⁄₂ [dozen] sherry glasses	*1 dozen white wines*
2 dozen finger bowls	*(green to sample)[205]*

The saltcellars, punch glasses, and green wineglasses were less expensive than the other items in the order. They were, therefore, probably not in the Russian pattern. Instead, they must have been the hobnail salts, strawberry-diamond punch glasses, and Lincoln-pattern green wineglasses.

FIG. 41. The engraved insignia on the goblet in figure 43, part of the glassware service first ordered by President Benjamin Harrison in 1891. Unlike the insignia on earlier pieces, the eagle's head here faces its left. Rather than sitting on a shield, as does the eagle on the Jackson service, this eagle bears the shield across its breast.

LEFT: FIG. 42. Claret glass, sherry glass, decanter, wineglass, and champagne glass from the Russian-pattern service first ordered by President Benjamin Harrison in 1891. Ht. of decanter 11⁵/₈″.

ABOVE: FIG. 43. Russian-pattern goblet, water bottle, Apollinaris tumbler, ice cream plate, finger bowl, and brandy-and-soda tumbler from the Harrison service. Ht. of water bottle 8¹/₄″.

That year the McKinleys received as a gift a magnificent cut-glass punch bowl created especially for the President by the Libbey Glass Company of Toledo, Ohio. J. D. Robinson, secretary of the glass company, was the son-in-law of a friend of the President's. The Libbey cutting shop foreman worked out a design based on stars and stripes within a shield. The 50-pound bowl was presented to President and Mrs. McKinley at the end of November.[206] It was apparently removed by Mrs. McKinley with her own furniture when she left the White House in 1901, and it has since disappeared. The glass company made a duplicate at the same time. It was common practice to make two presentation pieces simultaneously, in case one was broken during the cutting. Libbey eventually sold the second bowl; it is now in the collection of the High Museum, in Atlanta, Georgia.

On April 18, 1900, Col. Theodore Bingham, then the commissioner in charge of the White House, wrote to Dulin & Martin (who had taken over Beveridge's business after his death) to order some "Harrison" plates and several types of cut glass.[207] He wanted delivery in six weeks, a short notice for glass to be specially cut and engraved. The letter requested

FIG. 44. Saltcellar cut in a hobnail pattern. T. G. Hawkes & Company or C. Dorflinger & Sons, 1891–1910. Ht. 1 1/8". One order, that of 1898 from Hawkes, includes a dozen saltcellars; but 24 are on the 1901 inventory, so another dozen must have been ordered from Hawkes or Dorflinger.

2 Berry dishes, cut glass	*$10 each*
12 Ice Cream plates, Russian cut glass,	*62.00*
12 Punch glasses, cut glass	*12.50*
24 Burgundy glasses, ruby at	*41.25 per doz*
12 White wines, cut glass, green	*41.25*
18 Olive dishes, cut glass	*37.50 per doz.*

From the descriptions it would seem that only the ice cream plates were in the Russian pattern. The punch glasses must have been like the strawberry-diamond ones ordered previously for the same price. The Burgundy glasses and wineglasses, both colored and in shapes not listed in previous Russian-pattern orders, doubtless were a further reorder of the Lincoln-pattern glass. The berry dishes (probably circular 8-inch or 9-inch bowls) and the olive dishes (with no pattern given) were probably inexpensive diamond cuttings. Two of the olive dishes (fig. 49), slightly different in pattern, remain in the White House. One of them has the Hawkes trademark. All the glass was probably made by Hawkes, since that firm had filled the last Dulin & Martin order for ice cream plates at the same price. Breakage of the ice cream plates must have been considerable, because in June 1901 Dulin & Martin supplied another dozen at the same price.[208] These too were probably from Hawkes. Most of the ice cream plates remaining in the White House bear the Hawkes trademark (page 107). A close examination of one of the White House plates with the Hawkes trademark and of a sample plate from the same service belonging to Christian Dorflinger's granddaughter shows no apparent difference in the cutting and only minor differences in the engraved insignia. Such a comparison underscores the difficulty of distinguishing between the glasses from different White House orders.

In 1901 a detailed inventory of the White House was made under Colonel Bingham's supervision. For the first time the glass was listed with a President's name.[209] The following items are described as "Purchased during the administration of President Benjamin Harrison, Coat-of-arms engraved." The shapes and quantities listed are about what was purchased in 1891 and later, allowing for some breakage.

OPPOSITE: *In the East Room, Lincoln- and Russian-pattern stemware sparkles on a table prepared for a state dinner on February 24, 1902. President Theodore Roosevelt was host for the occasion honoring Prince Henry of Prussia.*

82 bowls, finger	*81 plates, ice cream*
83 glasses, sherry, stem	*92 glasses, claret*

85 bowls, champagne   69 tumblers, champagne
81 glasses, burgundy   97 goblets
12 plates, ice cream

The next few entries are probably also part of the cut glass purchased in the
1880s and 1890s, although no further description accompanies them. They include

7 decanters	24 saltcellars
26 bottles, water	1 dish, celery, flat
83 glasses, punch, without coat of arms	7 glasses cracked
8 claret jugs, silver topped	6 dishes, berry, oblong
4 decanters, cut glass	1 bowl, rose
3 bowls, rose	7 dishes, olive, with handles
6 dishes, berry	18 dishes, olive
2 dishes, olive without handles	

Because the other punch glasses had a coat of arms, these, without the arms, are
strawberry-diamond ones. Some of the claret jugs with silver tops are probably the
six "flagons" bought in 1894. Some of the water bottles and decanters must be part
of the Harrison Russian set. The 24 saltcellars (fig. 44) are the hobnail ones still in
the White House, although orders for only the dozen bought in 1898 remain. Three
of the rose bowls are still in the White House, but the flat celery dish and the berry
dishes cannot be identified—unless one is the surviving shallow oval dish (fig. 47).

106

Seventeen of the next 20 entries on the list are described as "Coat of arms engraved on same." Most likely they matched the Lincoln-pattern set. The Madeira and port glasses and the stoppers are not designated as "Coat of arms engraved" in the original, but they are listed immediately following those so described, and they are shapes that belong to that set.

Twin hawks within a trefoil serve as an early trademark of T. G. Hawkes & Company. Registered symbols standing for manufacturers appeared on U. S. cut glassware in the 1890s. Amid a growing proliferation of glasshouses, trademarks helped assure buyers that manufacturers stood behind their products and their reputations.

40 boules, water.	*24 glasses burgundy, ruby*
63 glasses, burgundy, ruby	*5 goblets*
19 glasses, liqueur	*56 dishes, sauce*
19 bowls, finger	*2 bowls, sugar*
11 plates, ice cream	*60 glasses, sherry*
7 glasses, Rhine wine	*4 glasses, celery, tall*
28 glasses, claret	*25 glasses, punch, tall, with handles*
19 decanters, tall	*54 glasses, madeira, ruby*
81 glasses, sauterne, green	*63 glasses, port*
12 glasses, sauterne, green	*10 stoppers, cut glass*

The largest quantities are of the colored wineglasses and the sherry glasses. These evidently were still being used, since there had been a recent reorder. The shallow Lincoln-pattern bowl (fig. 30) now in the White House may have been one of the sauce dishes, but this is the first such description. The compotes or cake stands are not listed in the above section, although some are in the inventory.

In the next most numerous group the glasses are described as "engraved with vine" or "engraved with vine, odd." Probably these were the remains of the first coat-of-arms set, the one used from Jackson's term until Pierce's. This group may also have included the vine-engraved set perhaps ordered by Pierce, and the ivy-engraved set that Grant may have ordered. In context, the designation "odd" that appears with the first sherry and liqueur glasses could indicate a mixture of types; it could be a reference to one of the sets with no insignia; or it could be a misspelling of "old," a term that appears in several entries. The group is listed as

16 glasses, sherry, odd	*26 glasses, liqueur, stem, odd*
13 glasses, sauterne, stem	*11 glasses, sauterne, stem*
18 glasses, sauterne, stem	*64 glasses, white wine*
29 glasses, claret	*25 glasses, claret*
4 glasses, Rhine wine	*27 glasses, burgundy*
22 glasses, claret	*38 bowls, finger*
23 bottles, water	*3 dishes, berry*
6 decanters with handles	*6 decanters*
1 decanter, old	*12 dishes, celery*

The next group is designated "Roman border." The label refers to a set of stemware (fig. 46) for which no order has been found. The last items in this portion of the inventory, the romers, are puzzling. A romer was an unusual type of European wineglass. The 17th-century term was rarely applied to American glass; therefore, it is difficult to identify the shape of glasses here listed as romers.

> *24 glasses, liqueur, engraved, Roman border, old*
> *64 glasses, sherry, engraved, Roman, old*
> *43 glasses, champagne, engraved, Roman, old*

14 glasses, claret, engraved, Roman border
35 glasses, burgundy, engraved, Roman border
25 romers, engraved with border

The last group is without designation, although some items—including individual saltcellars (fig. 48)—can be identified:

1 bottle, water, plain   *3 decanters with handles*
71 goblets, plain   *4 vases*
3 dishes, berry, high   *11 saltcellars, individual*
12 goblets, engraved   *24 iridescent bonbon dishes*
24 cocktail glasses, engraved with star   *2 bowls, large, used with gilt*
20 glasses, Roman punch   *plateau in dining room*
3 stands, cake, high

The final entry refers to the large "jelly glasses" bought for the plateau by President Pierce. Although not all the glassware on this inventory is still in the White House, the document is helpful in identifying the three major 19th-century sets.

Theodore Roosevelt

In 1901 President McKinley was assassinated at the Pan-American Exposition, in Buffalo. He was succeeded by Vice President Theodore Roosevelt. Roosevelt and his wife, Edith, entertained frequently, and more exclusively. Said a contemporary:

From the first Mrs. Roosevelt realized that radical reform was necessary at the White House. The looseness of the invitation system led her to inaugurate her present rigid social regime. . . . Each season the corps diplomatique, the cabinet, and members of the Supreme Court must be invited to dine at the White House. And a series of receptions are de rigueur at which Washington official society is invited to meet, respectively, the diplomats, the judiciary, the army and navy, and members of Congress.[210]

Edith Roosevelt thought that both the glass and china needed replacing. She decided on an entirely new design for the state china, which for the first time was English porcelain rather than French, but she continued to reorder the existing glassware. She ordered both glass and china from the Van Heusen Charles Company, of Albany, New York. The correspondence regarding the glassware order began with a letter dated December 2, 1901, from Charles Van Heusen. He wrote, "I have not received the sample of claret glass and would you be kind enough also to send a finger bowl? That was badly broken, and in order to get the right size I will have to have a whole piece."[211] On March 22, 1902, Van Heusen wrote again:

Would you be kind enough to inform Mrs. Roosevelt that the glass service has been completed, and we will forward it at once to the White House. We have had the very best workmen in the country do this work, and I am sure Mrs. Roosevelt will find it a very beautiful and very perfect lot. . . .[212]

The voucher for the 1902 order is not in the National Archives, so we have no complete listing. The inventory taken June 30, 1903, however, was more detailed than former ones. It lists, in the private dining room, goblets, claret glasses, cordial glasses, handled punch cups, plates, and finger bowls, all cut glass and all received July 2, 1902, from the Van Heusen Charles Company. Only a dozen or a dozen and a half of each shape are noted, so the order was evidently a small one.

It would seem that this was a reorder of the Russian pattern, but correspondence between Edwin A. Barber, curator of the Pennsylvania Museum (now the Philadelphia Museum of Art), and William Dorflinger indicates that it was instead the Lincoln-pattern glassware. Barber wrote, "I have just procured a photograph of . . . the glass service . . . used at present at the White House, and I understand that this was made by your firm."[213] Dorflinger responded, "We have just made some stemware for the White House, which corresponds to the description you gave us. . . . We have made this set at various times, but have not always made it."[214]

The following month Dorflinger sent to the museum a Russian-pattern tumbler and a Lincoln-pattern wineglass and a note: "Referring to the matter of glass [for] the White House, we are sending . . . two samples. The tumbler . . . was of a set which was made up for the White House about 1888 or 89 during President Harrison's administration. The claret glass . . . is of the set which they are using at the present time."[215] The museum still has both of these glasses; judging from Dorflinger's comments, the firm had not supplied the Russian pattern to any President other than Harrison. The Lincoln-pattern sample glasses that have descended in the Dorflinger family are all in the shapes ordered in 1902, a coincidence that may indicate that these glasses were factory samples from 1902 rather than from 1861, the year of the original order. A fire in 1892 at the Dorflinger plant in White Mills destroyed the early factory records and may have also destroyed the earlier samples.

The 1903 inventory mentioned above is one of the most detailed ones.[216] It was supervised by Col. T. W. Symons, now the officer in charge of the White House. A few more pieces are listed as being in the private dining room, including ice cream plates, saltcellars, and pitchers, all cut glass, and more pitchers that are not cut. A dozen inexpensive goblets bought in February 1903 from Dulin & Martin are also listed as being in the room. The rest of the glassware is listed as being in the basement, where it was stored. The Russian-pattern service is grouped as "Coat of arms" glass; and no new purchases since 1901 are listed, although 25 glasses are described as "damaged and worthless" and disposed of since the last inventory. The basic totals had changed little since 1901.

The Roosevelts were a lively family with four young sons and two daughters. The older daughter, Alice, was married with great ceremony in 1906, and the younger, Ethel, made her debut with a dance at the White House in 1908. For both occasions much glassware was required.

Mrs. Roosevelt apparently decided to add to the Russian set rather than to the Lincoln-pattern set. Twenty-one finger bowls, 24 goblets and 23 "Ice Creams" were delivered by Van Heusen in March 1906.[217] Judging from the prices, these were all in the more expensive Russian pattern. In May three more finger bowls and a plate arrived. The White House wrote to four local retailers, Galt & Brother, Harris & Shafer, Dulin & Martin, and Charles R. Edmonston, asking for bids on a few dozen water glasses, Apollinaris glasses, champagne glasses, sherry glasses, and finger bowls "to match sets now in use."[218] Dulin & Martin replied that they had sent the samples to "the factory" and would send in a bid soon. Their bid, probably from Hawkes, was $867. Edmonston's bid was $860, and Galt & Brother's was $655.05. The low bidder, Galt, received the order. Galt had specified: "The above glasses to be made by the same concern which furnished the original sets, *and for which we are*

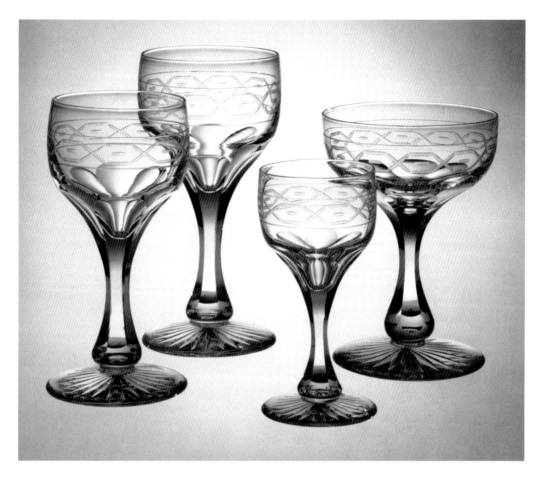

LEFT: *FIG. 45. Cut-glass and sterling silver jug, probably purchased in 1894. United States, silver by R. Wallace and Sons. Ht. 9¹/₄". These jugs are called "flagons" on the invoice. Since they have no fitted stoppers, they were more likely intended for serving water than for serving wine.*

ABOVE: *FIG. 46. Claret, burgundy, sherry, and champagne glasses, engraved with "Roman border." United States, 1890–1900. Ht. of tallest 5⁵/₈". This set is on the 1901 inventory, but no invoice has been found.*

RIGHT: FIG. 47. *Celery or berry dish. United States, ca. 1900. Width 8⁷⁄₈".* *This could be either the celery dish or one of the "berry dishes, oblong" in the 1901 inventory.*

FIG. 48. *Individual saltcellars. United States, 1890–1900. Width of top saltcellar 2¹⁄₄". These are on the 1901 inventory. They were for family rather than formal use, since there were not more than a dozen of them.*

now exclusive agents in Washington." This was the Dorflinger company of White Mills, but once again the glasses were engraved by Joseph Haselbauer. The Corning newspaper reported:

> *Joseph F. Haselbauer and son Frederick, of 84 West Third Street, are engaged in engraving a number of pieces of glassware, belonging to what is known as the "President Harrison set" at the White House, the engraving of the original set having been done in Corning. Since coming to this country, about 40 years ago, Joseph Haselbauer has worked on nearly every order for cut glass that has gone to the White House.[219]*

Apparently, Joseph Haselbauer and his son, Frederick, traveled to White Mills to do some of this work. Louis J. Dorflinger's diary places them at Dorflinger's in January and again in June 1906 to work on the presidential order. The glass was delivered October 31, and Galt was requested to submit samples of whiskey glasses to match. The firm sent a whiskey tumbler and a larger brandy-and-soda tumbler. Mrs. Roosevelt ordered three dozen brandy-and-soda tumblers (fig. 43),[220] the first time this shape had been purchased for the White House. They were $75 per dozen, $25 more than the price per dozen of the smaller whiskey tumblers.

The Roosevelts, for the extent to which they entertained, ordered little glassware. Theodore Roosevelt rarely drank hard liquor, according to his aide Archibald Butt. The President did enjoy occasional mint juleps, and he drank wine in small amounts at lunch or dinner.[221] Butt recorded: "I made the contract for the state dinners to-day, awarding them to Rauscher at seven dollars and seventy-five cents a plate, he to furnish everything, dishes, glasses, linen, all except the plates and the champagne and the cigars."[222] The dishes and glasses could not have been those actually used by guests, because Mrs. Roosevelt had bought a new set of china for that purpose, and the glasses that appear in period photographs of the dining room were a mixture of the Lincoln-pattern and Russian-pattern sets.

Butt said that the President insisted on buying his own wine and cigars because he wanted only the best for the White House. "It goes against the grain of both Mrs. Roosevelt and the President to have their state dinners served by any one else than the White House chef," wrote Butt, "but the fact of the matter is that the accommodations of the White House hardly admit of a dinner for a hundred people."[223] In his letters to his mother and his sister, Butt, a bachelor, described a number of White House social affairs that he was duty-bound to attend:

FIG. 49. Olive dishes. T. G. Hawkes & Company, Corning, 1900. Width of dish on left 6⁷/₈". The Hawkes trademark — not visible in the photograph — is stamped on the dish on the right.

> *At the state dinners the guests assemble in the East Room and a much greater degree of formality is necessary at these dinners than others. . . . Most people think that . . . state dinners . . . are paid for by the State. I found that Mrs. Taft thought so, too, and it was somewhat of a shock when I told her that the President has to pay for every dinner out of his own pay as President [not the case today — AUTHOR]. . . . [S]ome President's state dinners have been very meagre in consequence, but the Roosevelts spend more money on their dinners than has ever been spent on them before in any past administration.[224]*

Major Butt was given the responsibility of smashing the chipped china and glass that had accumulated. He described the task in two letters:

> *I had rather an interesting time the last few days looking over the china at the White House with a view to destroying all that is chipped or broken. . . . Mrs. Roosevelt does not want it sold at auction, for she thinks this method cheapens the White House. . . . In former years it was regarded as the property of the mistress of the White House, who would give it away . . . but Mrs. R. thinks that it should never be given away. . . . If it were sold by private bids it would create an awful howl in the press should it become known, and so I convinced all concerned that it should be broken up and scattered in the river, which will be done. When I think how I should value even one piece of it, it hurts to smash it, but I am sure it is the only right thing to do. . . .[225]*

In a later letter Butt described how he actually smashed the china and glass. He removed several broken pieces for himself and the First Lady's social secretary. For Mrs. Roosevelt he saved several chipped plates from the Wedgwood service she had chosen for the White House.[226] Probably at this time he gave an engraved decanter from the Jackson-pattern set to Ethel Roosevelt, whose daughter still has it.

*A drawing on an 1882 map of Corning advertises T. G. Hawkes &
Company. Access to river and rail for shipping and to Pennsylvania
coal for furnaces made Corning a glass manufacturing center.*

William H. Taft

President Taft was inaugurated in 1909. Mrs. Taft, believing it ridiculous to change china and glass patterns frequently, decided to use Edith Roosevelt's china and the Harrison glassware. Replacements for the Russian-pattern service were made in 1910 and 1912, but both orders were small, involving only a few dozen glasses. Both orders went through the retail firm of Dulin & Martin. According to records of the Dorflinger factory for 1912, the 1912 order was made there.[227] Mrs. Taft's decision to use the existing china was soon overturned by the second Mrs. Wilson, but the Russian-pattern service of glass was destined to be used as the state service until 1937, when it was replaced by another pattern.

Inventories after the turn of the century were taken yearly and in a more orderly fashion. From 1910 to 1917 few glass purchases were made. The Tafts entertained as elaborately as had the Roosevelts, but during the Taft administration, a decision was made to stop reordering the cut punch glasses. Instead, several hundred inexpensive pressed punch glasses and three pressed punch bowls were added for serving fruit punch at receptions. Another new form added to the pantry was the cocktail glass. Two dozen star-engraved cocktail glasses and a dozen leaf-bordered ones appear on early 20th-century inventories, probably for family use and for small dinner parties.

Woodrow Wilson

Woodrow Wilson was inaugurated March 4, 1913. Ellen Axson Wilson was a reserved woman who attached little importance to public position or glamorous entertaining. The once elaborate White House dinners and receptions now became small, sedate affairs. The most glittering social event of Wilson's first term was his daughter Jessie's wedding in the East Room in November 1913. In the summer of 1914 Mrs. Wilson died, and for the following year White House entertaining was curtailed. White House dinners then were characterized as "long and dull."[228]

Late in 1915 Wilson married Edith Bolling Galt and social life at the White House grew livelier. She was the widow of Norman Galt, from whom she had inherited the family jewelry business. Galt & Brother was the Washington firm that had earlier supplied the White House with glass from Dorflinger. In 1917 President and Mrs. Wilson decided to purchase new glass and china, both to be of American manufacture. Their wishes were relayed to Dr. George Frederick Kunz, a gemologist and an officer of Tiffany & Company in New York City. Kunz requested a copy of the Presidential Seal. In June 1917 he acknowledged its receipt by letter, concluding: "We hope to send the porcelains and the glass, with the arms engraved on them, sometime this week."[229] The company did not ship the glassware until September. Apparently, Dr. Kunz had experienced difficulty in having it made. The company, he wrote, was sending "a drinking glass which has been specially made, following the lines of certain of the other glasses and the device added." He continued, "As this glass required special making, it was not ready at the time that we sent the plate."[230] Neither the glass tumbler nor the plate must have pleased the Wilsons. Col. William W. Harts, commissioner of public buildings, passed their ideas to an intermediary for transmission to Kunz:

> *In regard to the glass ware, the President liked the glass ware for every purpose except drinking, the bell mouth not being a comfortable shape to use owing to the likelihood of spilling water while using the tumbler. This is*

115

FIG. 50. Cut-glass jar with silver top engraved "President's House 1901." United States, 1901. Ht. 4¹/₂". This jar was probably intended for use on a vanity. No order for it has yet been found.

sufficient objection to the bell shape. Mrs. Wilson liked the tumbler in every respect except the marking. She preferred a wreath of leaves, open at the top, with the President's seal instead of the modified eagle within the wreath. The cutting, too, on the tumbler was so fine in detail that the general effect was lost. It would seem necessary to look further for glass ware, although in general the kind of light glass with dignified cutting seemed to please both the President and Mrs. Wilson. . . . I promised to have . . . another article of glass ware to illustrate these suggestions . . . Could you see whether it would be agreeable for Tiffany and Company to prepare these samples? . . . I hope too that Dr. Kunz will see the desirability of giving us his best rates on account of the large quantity. . . .[231]

On October 11 Dr. Kunz and his colleagues at Tiffany sent three more sample glasses, along with the rejected one for comparison.[232] The three new glasses were all stemware. The Wilsons' reaction to these glasses must have been negative, for no new glassware was ordered. The negotiations with Tiffany dragged on until the end of the year. The Wilsons finally ordered a new porcelain dinner service from Lenox, of Trenton, New Jersey, instead of from the New York firm. Tiffany's records of the negotiations no longer exist, so there is little chance of finding a record of the rejected designs or of which glass company produced them.

In July Colonel Harts had asked several firms to submit sealed bids for new glassware in the Russian pattern. Two dozen each of goblets, finger bowls, and sherry glasses, and four dozen Apollinaris tumblers and champagne glasses were needed.[233] All were purchased from Dulin & Martin, the Washington retailer. Perhaps for reasons of economy, the glass was bought in twice-a-month installments. The first installment, on October 22, consisted of two dozen finger bowls. The final one—two dozen champagne glasses—was dated February 18, 1918.[234] This was the last order of the Russian pattern, and according to Dorflinger family tradition, it had been made in White Mills just as the first one had.

After April 7, 1917, when the United States entered World War I, all White House receptions and dinners were canceled, making the Wilsons' concern over the glass and china surprising. Following the Armistice in November 1918 the Wilsons did not resume entertaining; the President's travels and subsequent illness prohibited it. The ratification of the 18th Amendment in January of 1919 also diminished the demand for glassware in the White House. The amendment, which proscribed the manufacture, importation, and sale of alcoholic beverages within the United States, did not take effect until the following year. When it did, it was observed in spirit—or lack thereof—even in private during Wilson's last year in office. After the 1918 shipments no new glass or china was ordered during the remainder of Wilson's term.

20th-Century Glass

During World War I the American glass factories that had made fine tableware suffered. Lead, a principal ingredient of fine glass, was in short supply. Heavily cut glass, popular for two decades after 1890, had gone out of fashion. Lighter weight glass, with less elaborate cutting and engraving, had gained popularity. Thus many companies, with less work for their cutters and engravers, were forced to close.

Prohibition brought new problems to the glass industry in the 1920s. The market for expensive stemware sets nearly disappeared, although water and iced tea glasses were still in demand. The Depression in the 1930s reduced the demand for luxury glass even more. When the Franklin Roosevelts decided to order a new set of stemware in 1937, lightweight glass was still popular. The set they chose exemplified the taste of this period. It had straight lines, minimal cutting, and a very simple version of the U. S. coat of arms. The service remained in use for state affairs for only 24 years, a shorter time than had the two previous services. This was not so much due to fashion as to the difficulty of obtaining replacements. The skilled craftsmen who had produced the glassware had grown old, and few young craftsmen were being trained. Cut and engraved table glass was a product of a labor-intensive industry that had nearly disappeared in the United States by the 1950s. The White House service chosen in 1961 and still in use today has no cut or engraved decoration.

FIG. 51. Strawberry Mansion urn. Steuben Glass, Corning, New York, 1939. Ht. 12 1/2". Made for the Federal Building at the World's Fair in New York and transferred to the White House in 1941.

Warren G. Harding to the Present

Warren G. Harding was inaugurated in 1921. In May of that year Mrs. Harding received a gift set of gilded glassware in the Dragon pattern (figs. 52, 53). The presentation was made by the manufacturer, the Central Glass Works, of Wheeling, West Virginia. On May 26 a trade publication announced the gift to the public:

Of special interest to lovers of beautiful glassware are the exquisite sets that now grace the tables at the executive mansions of President Harding at Washington and Governor Morgan at Charlestown. They were designed and executed by the Central Glass Works of Wheeling, West Virginia and are

119

*considered far superior in design and workmanship to anything yet pro-
duced in America. Mrs. Harding selected the Dragon design which has been
made up in 336 pieces. . . . This set is etched and filled in with gold. It is gold-
rimmed and gold-stemmed and each piece has a 35-point star on the bottom.
The set goes with the historic White House gold service and will be used only
on state occasions. It is Mrs. Harding's own property and will be taken away
with her. . . . The set comprises drinking pieces, goblets, sherberts, com-
ports, oyster cocktail glasses, plates, oil and vinegar, cream and sugar, salt
and pepper and innumerable other glass accessories essential to a glass dining room set. . . . It is not generally known, but foreign glassware has always
been used at the White House table. The installation of the American product
to replace the foreign-made article has been heralded with considerable ac-
claim by glass manufacturers of the United States.*[235]

The writer was, of course, incorrect in stating that foreign glassware had
"always been used at the White House table." Beginning with Monroe's purchase,
all state services had been American. Mrs. Harding's gilded service was used at state
dinners, now larger than those of the past. As many as 104 people were served at a
specially erected horseshoe table.

The Hardings did a great deal of entertaining, but they appear not to have purchased any glassware for the White House. They owned a set of cut glassware made
by H. P. Sinclaire, of Corning, a lightweight pattern called "Adam #2,"[236] and they
had a plainer service of Sinclaire glass for everyday use. Both Sinclaire sets, however, were personal possessions not used in the White House.

One Corning publication stated in 1948 that the Hunt Glass Company of Corning, a cutting shop, had filled a large stemware order for President Harding in
1920.[237] But Harding was not yet President. Furthermore, though the Hardings are
known to have served liquor at their private parties in the White House,[238] it is not
likely that they would have publicly ordered new wineglasses during Prohibition.

Several local cutters in Corning claimed to remember a large punch bowl made
for the White House in the 1920s at H. P. Sinclaire & Company.[239] As with the stemware order, no corroborating evidence for it has yet been found.

President Harding died in August 1923 and was succeeded by Vice President
Calvin Coolidge. Prohibition was strictly observed in the administrations of Coolidge and of his successor, Herbert Hoover. Between December and February there
were four state dinners, each for about a hundred guests: the Cabinet dinner, the
diplomatic dinner, the Supreme Court dinner, and the House speaker's dinner. All
were white-tie occasions. During the same period there were five large state receptions for about 3,500 guests each, in addition to the traditional New Year's
reception. At these winter affairs the President received members of the diplomatic
corps, the judiciary, Congress, and officers of the Army and Navy. The winter social
season was followed by two Lenten musicales and several spring garden parties.[240]

No new glassware was added by the Coolidges. The Hoovers, however, chose
some glass cream-soup bowls and saucers. They were ordered through B. Altman &
Company, of New York, in 1929 and 1930. The open-stock pieces were cut in a diamond pattern by Bryce Brothers, of Mount Pleasant, Pennsylvania.

In 1932 President and Mrs. Hoover presided at the last New Year's Day reception held at the White House. Several thousand guests filed through in the receiving
line. The whole process was so exhausting that the Hoovers allowed the tradition
begun by George Washington to die quietly the following year.

Franklin D. Roosevelt took office in 1933 in the depths of the Great Depression. Mrs. Roosevelt found that both the dinner service purchased by the Wilsons in 1918 and the glass service originally ordered by the Harrisons in 1891 were still in use, although the Russian-pattern decanters had been sent to storage because of Prohibition. Mrs. Roosevelt ordered a new set of china in 1934 at a cost of $9,000. Although it seemed a tremendous sum, Mrs. Roosevelt justified the expense. It was cheaper to order a new set of 1,722 pieces, she said, than to continue to have replacements specially made. Besides, it would provide employment. This order too went to the Lenox factory in Trenton;[241] it would have been unthinkable to buy foreign dinnerware at such a time.

When Prohibition was repealed in 1933, the Roosevelts began to serve wine at state dinners, using the Russian- and the Lincoln-pattern sets together. A press release from the White House indicated that no distilled liquors would be served at official entertainments—only wine, and that would be American if possible.[242]

Mrs. Roosevelt also ordered more cut glassware for family use (fig. 56), the same pattern the Hoovers had selected in 1929. It was ordered through Garfinckel's, a Washington store, instead of B. Altman, the store that had handled Mrs. Hoover's purchase.[243] The Roosevelts' first order for the informal tableware was placed in 1933, and the glass was repeatedly reordered. The pattern is a simple diamond cutting, and the cost was nominal, averaging about a dollar an item. Water goblets, tumblers in two sizes, cordial glasses, juice glasses, sherbets in two sizes, finger bowls, and berry or soup bowls with saucers were all in use until the 1950s.

In 1937 the Roosevelts decided to buy new state glassware. It was ordered through Martin's China and Glassware, a Washington retailer, and manufactured by T. G. Hawkes & Company. The Roosevelts chose a pattern that Hawkes had marketed as "Venetian," but which the firm renamed "White House." The coat of arms was added to the pattern for the Roosevelts (fig 59).

Henrietta Nesbitt, the White House housekeeper, recalled that Hawkes had trouble finding enough experienced engravers. According to the recollections of former employees and to company records, Edward Palme and Joseph Sidot, two of the older engravers, did most of the work on the Roosevelt order. The first samples were not faithful to the design that was requested, so President Roosevelt sent them back.[244] The insignia that was finally engraved (fig. 60) was a simplified version of the one designed in 1861 for the Lincolns.

According to Miss Nesbitt, President Roosevelt had intended to spend no more than $60 a dozen for the stemware, so the choices were limited. The blanks used by Hawkes for the set, from the Tiffin Glass Company, of Tiffin, Ohio, were of a special formula made to Hawkes's specifications. Ten dozen each of goblets and finger bowls were ordered late in 1937 for $95 a dozen. Although the invoice for the remainder of the set has not been located, wineglasses must have been ordered at the same time. This was a much larger order than previous ones, which had usually consisted of four to six dozen of each shape.

In April 1939 the Hawkes company provided estimates for hollow-stem champagne glasses in a trumpet shape at $100 a dozen, plus $60 more for the engraving of the insignia; a saucerlike shape at $80 a dozen, or $140 with engraving, and special saucer champagnes (for which a special stem mold would be made) at $160 or $216 a dozen. The hollow-stem champagnes were never ordered, probably because they were so expensive. Plain saucer champagne glasses were bought instead.[245] The following year cordial glasses were ordered to match, and in 1941 smaller wineglasses and sherry glasses were purchased. In 1946 champagne glasses and cordial glasses, without the engraved insignia but with matching cutting, were bought by the Trumans, and in 1947 and 1950 the goblets and finger bowls were reordered.[246]

Vice President Harry S. Truman had become President upon Roosevelt's death in 1945. During Truman's administration obtaining replacements for the set became difficult. In the 1930s when the glass had first been ordered, only a few firms were producing hand-cut and specially engraved stemware, in contrast to the several hundred that were doing such work when the Russian-pattern set was ordered in the 1890s. After World War II only Steuben Glass and T. G. Hawkes & Company, both in Corning, were producing highest quality hand-blown lead-glass stemware with special cutting and engraving. As demand dropped, the glass became much more expensive, leading to a further decline in demand and to a reduced supply. In 1955 replacements were ordered from Hawkes—the last to be purchased from the firm.

Earlier the White House had acquired more glassware free of charge. When the New York World's Fair of 1939–1940 closed, pieces that had been specially made by the Libbey Glass Company for the Federal Building were offered to the White House (figs. 54, 55). The glass was acid-etched with a stylized version of the Great Seal. The blanks for this set, with pressed stems, were designed by Edwin Fuerst, Libbey's chief designer, and by Walter Dorwin Teague, an influential free-lance designer of the 1930s. The shape was called "Embassy" by Libbey. There were eight sizes of stemware and three sizes of tumblers in the set, as well as finger bowls that have since disappeared. The set included nine or ten dozen of each item—enough to serve large parties—though the pieces were used mostly at formal luncheons.[247]

Eight large Steuben vases (fig. 51) that had also been in the Federal Building were part of the gift, though not all remain. They were produced in the Strawberry Mansion pattern. Designed in 1931, the pattern was inspired by an 18th-century continental goblet; it was named after Strawberry Mansion, an 18th-century house in Philadelphia's Fairmount Park.

The last of the eagle-engraved sets of glasses acquired in the 1940s was ordered for the presidential yacht U.S.S. *Williamsburg* in 1945 (fig. 61). Steuben Glass filled the special order. Champagne glasses in two shapes, white wine glasses, cordials, old-fashioneds, cocktail glasses, highball glasses, pilsners, jiggers, decanters, cocktail shakers, ashtrays, cigarette boxes, and a pitcher, all engraved with an American eagle surrounded by stars, made up this set. When the *Williamsburg* was decommissioned in 1953, the Navy gave three of the remaining glasses to the White House. The rest of the set was disposed of.[248]

Dwight D. Eisenhower began his first term on January 20, 1953. When replacements for the FDR set of glassware were needed in 1955, they were supplied by Hawkes. In 1958 during Eisenhower's second term, however, Hawkes no longer had engravers who could do the work, so the White House ordered the replacements through an importing firm, Royal York China. The pieces were made in West Germany—marking the first time since President Madison's term that the White House had purchased European glass (fig. 58) for a state service. Four dozen each of goblets, champagne glasses, red- and white-wine glasses, sherry glasses, and finger bowls were ordered at an unusually low price: $35 a dozen for the stemware and $47 a dozen for the finger bowls. On these pieces the insignia was acid-etched (fig. 57) rather than copper-wheel engraved, accounting for the low price. A letter from William Graham, of Royal York China, recommended the acid-etching technique:

> *On close examination of the samples [that the White House wanted to have matched], I find them to be all Wheel Engraving and not the flat etching like*

the State Dept. uses from me. . . . These Wheel Engravings are very difficult to do especially on the small sizes and will cost $4.00 to $5.00 a piece. . . . The etchings will look just as well and at more than a yard distant would need an expert to tell the difference.[249]

When the Kennedys entered the White House in January 1961, Mrs. Kennedy continued to use the Truman china, but she ordered new glassware. The Kennedys were grateful to the voters of West Virginia, for it had been JFK's big win in that state's primary that made him a viable candidate for the Democratic nomination. Because the economy of the state was severely depressed, Mrs. Kennedy chose glass made in West Virginia, a major glass-producing state, for the White House.

For the first time since the Pierce administration, an open-stock pattern with no engraving (fig. 63) was ordered for use at state dinners. Six dozen each of water goblets, red- and white-wine glasses, tulip-shaped champagne glasses, and finger bowls were ordered from Morgantown Glassware Guild in May 1961.[250] To a suggestion that more elaborate glassware would be appropriate, Mrs. Kennedy replied, "I really love my West Virginia wineglasses. . . . Also, I really don't mind having plain glasses without a seal. It is almost a relief. Our flatware and china are all engraved."[251]

At $11.60 a dozen the pieces made up the least expensive state service ever ordered. The glass itself contains no lead and is machine-made rather than handblown. These two factors account for the low price. Lead glass, commonly advertised as "crystal" and used for all the previous White House services, is finer in quality and more sparkling than nonlead glass. The basic design of the new set was simple, relying on clean lines rather than decoration for its appeal. Several other American glass companies made similarly shaped glasses, including the Seneca Glass Company, also in Morgantown, which claims to have originated the shape. In fact, an identical design has been produced since 1886 by the French glass manufacturer Baccarat. Both Seneca and Baccarat produced the design in lead glassware, readily distinguishable from the Morgantown Glassware Guild's nonlead service.

Both the Morgantown Glass Guild and Fostoria, in Moundsville, West Virginia, which purchased the Morgantown molds and patterns when the former went out of business in 1971, marketed the pattern as "President's House." Fostoria supplied replacements to the set in 1974, during the Nixon administration, but that company too is now out of business. The molds for "President's House" were sold to the Lancaster Colony Company, which has never put the pattern into production.

In 1981 during the administration of Ronald Reagan, the White House received as a gift 131 pieces of Steuben's Strawberry Mansion glassware (fig. 62), which match the urns acquired after the World's Fair. The ornate set stands in striking contrast to the West Virginia glass. The Strawberry Mansion pieces, used for private lunches and dinners, are those most recently added to the White House collection.

Master Craftsmanship of Rare Beauty

FOR AMERICA'S "FIRST FAMILIES"

Harding Plate

Morgan Plate

Harding Tumbler

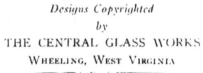

Designs Copyrighted
by
THE CENTRAL GLASS WORKS
WHEELING, WEST VIRGINIA

Harding Goblet

Morgan Tumbler

Harding Sherbet

Morgan Sherbet

LEFT: *An advertisement for the Central Glass Works displays pieces of a set of glassware the company presented in 1921 to Mrs. Warren G. Harding. Some of the gilded glassware can be seen in figures 52 and 53.*

ABOVE: *FIG. 52. Wineglass, water goblet, finger bowl, plate, and tumbler in the Dragon pattern. Central Glass Works, Wheeling, West Virginia, 1921. Ht. of tallest $7^5/_8$". Most of this glass is still in the Harding home in Ohio.*

RIGHT: *FIG. 53. Sherbet, champagne, and juice glasses in the Dragon pattern. Ht. of tallest 5". (Glassware in figures 52 and 53 a gift to the White House collection from the Harding Memorial Association, 1968.)*

LEFT: *FIG. 54. Sherry glass; Delmonico glass; goblet; and old-fashioned, highball, and Tom Collins tumblers in the Embassy shape. Libbey Glass Company, Toledo, Ohio, 1939. These and the ones shown in figure 55 were among those made for the dining room of the Federal Building at the World's Fair in New York. The shape was a stock item, but only the glassware made for the Federal Building had the acid-etched insignia. Ht. of tallest 8³/₄".*

ABOVE: *FIG. 55. Cocktail, dessert wine, dinner wine, cordial, and champagne glasses in the Embassy shape. Ht. of tallest 6⁷/₈". The Embassy glassware was transferred to the White House in 1941, following the World's Fair.*

FIG. 56. Sherbet glasses, finger bowl and plate, goblet, cordial glass, and tumbler. Bryce Brothers, Mount Pleasant, Pennsylvania, 1933–43. Ht. of tallest 5 $^1/_2$". This pattern had no engraving. First ordered by the Hoovers in 1929 and reordered by Mrs. Franklin Roosevelt in 1933, it was repeatedly reordered and used daily at the White House until the mid-1950s.

*Vice presidential candidate Harry S. Truman lunches with
President Franklin D. Roosevelt on the White House lawn in 1944.
Modern diamond-cut water goblets and late-19th-century hobnail
saltcellars are among the table appointments. The stemware
belongs to the service (opposite) purchased by the Roosevelts in
1933. This open-stock design had no pattern name, just a number
in Bryce Brothers factory records. Many American families set
their tables with the same glassware.*
ASSOCIATED PRESS

BELOW: FIG. 57. The acid-etched insignia on the wineglass in figure 58.

BOTTOM: FIG. 58. Wine and champagne glasses made in Germany for Royal York China, 1959. Ht. of tallest 5 5/8". Engraving, no longer available in the U. S., was costly even in Europe; thus, these pieces were acid-etched.

Flower-filled tables and formal place settings enhance the State Dining Room, prepared for guests of President Dwight D. Eisenhower. To increase the number of place settings, Theodore Roosevelt introduced the U-shaped table at the White House in 1902. His successor, William Howard Taft, put a rectangular table inside the horseshoe and increased the room's seating capacity by 30 percent. Glassware in the pattern illustrated in figure 59 graces the banquet setting.

ABOVE: FIG. 59. *Sherry glass, wineglass, goblet, champagne and cordial glasses, and finger bowl from the set first ordered by President and Mrs. Franklin Roosevelt in 1937. T. G. Hawkes & Company, Corning, 1937–55. Ht. of goblet 6".*

LEFT: FIG. 60. *A copper-wheel engraved insignia from the goblet in figure 59. A comparison of this insignia with the acid-etched one shown in figure 57 highlights the finely detailed work that can be achieved by wheel engraving.*

FIG. 61. *Sherry, champagne, and cocktail glass from the set ordered for the presidential yacht U.S.S. Williamsburg.* Steuben Glass, Corning, 1945. *The shape was a standard Steuben one, created by George Thompson, but the engraving was designed for the yacht. Ht. of tallest 6⁵/₁₆". These three glasses were transferred to the White House when the ship was decommissioned in 1953.*

*White House luncheon in the second-floor President's Dining Room
in March 1979 brings together President Jimmy Carter, Israeli Prime
Minister Menachem Begin, left, and Egyptian President Anwar Sadat.
The Carters entertained the two heads of state and their wives before
the signing of a peace treaty between Egypt and Israel. The unadorned
stemware selected by Mrs. John F. Kennedy accents the table.
The glassware remains the official state service today.*

COURTESY JIMMY CARTER LIBRARY

FIG. 62. *Sherry and wine glasses, goblet, finger bowl, plate, cordial and champagne glasses in the Strawberry Mansion pattern. Steuben Glass, Corning, 1931–39. Ht. of tallest 6". The glassware displays the talents of Corning's skillful copper-wheel engravers. The pattern was designed by Frederick Carder in 1931 and made originally in 1932, although it continued in production until the late 1930s. The set, given to the White House in 1981, includes nearly 20 of each shape. (Gift of Mr. and Mrs. Stanley F. Reed.)*

Elegant simplicity of the glassware below reflects the taste of Jacqueline Kennedy (left). She ordered the pattern in 1961, ending a White House tradition of engraved stemware.

ABBIE ROWE/WHITE HOUSE COLLECTION

The President and Mrs. Reagan
request the pleasure of the company of
The Secretary of State
at dinner
on Thursday, October 6, 1988
at 7:30 o'clock

Black Tie

On the occasion of the visit of
His Excellency
The President of the Republic of Mali
and Mrs. Traore

The Secretary of State

ABOVE: FIG. 63. *Wineglasses, tulip champagne glass, finger bowl, and goblet from the set originally ordered by President and Mrs. John F. Kennedy in 1961. Morgantown Glass Guild, Morgantown, West Virginia, 1961–71; or Fostoria Glass Company, Moundsville, West Virginia, 1974. Ht. of tallest 8 1/16". Many Americans purchased the same pattern. The clean lines of the glassware complement the ornate china and flatware (opposite) in the State Dining Room. The room is prepared for a state dinner given in 1988 by President and Mrs. Ronald Reagan for President and Mrs. Moussa Traore of Mali. At right, an invitation, place card, and dinner menu bearing the Presidential Seal attest to the formality of the occasion.*

RIGHT: WHITE HOUSE COLLECTION;
OPPOSITE: ERIK KVALSVIK/WHITE HOUSE COLLECTION

DINNER
Honoring His Excellency
The President of the Republic of Mali
and Mrs. Traore

Vegetable Terrine
and Lobster Medallions
Curry Mousseline
Fennel Leaves

Roast Loin of Veal with Wild Mushrooms
Semolina Gnocchis
Sautéed Zucchini

Radicchio and Endive Salad
Bel Paese Cheese

Cold Pumpkin Soufflé
with Candied Ginger
Petits Fours Sec

CHÂTEAU ST. JEAN Chardonnay 1986
STERLING WINERY LAKE Pinot Noir 1986
SCHRAMSBERG Crémant Demi Sec 1984

THE WHITE HOUSE
Thursday, October 6, 1988

136

Although Mrs. Lyndon Johnson did not replace the glassware ordered by the Kennedys, she purchased a new set of china for the White House. The design, produced by Castleton China, was largely inspired by the early-19th-century French porcelain ordered by Monroe and Jackson. Mrs. Ronald Reagan's more formal red-bordered service, ordered 13 years later from Lenox, is similar to the Lenox services of the Wilsons and the Roosevelts.

The Kennedy glassware service is equally suitable for use with both sets of china, and it complements informal as well as formal settings. The set is likely to be in use for some time. Its versatility has ensured its longevity.

The American glassware industry, however, fares less well. Only two companies, Lenox Crystal (formerly Bryce Brothers), of Mount Pleasant, Pennsylvania, and Steuben Glass, of Corning, New York, are making hand-blown lead-glass tableware. Steuben has nearly phased out its drinking glasses. The skills essential to making such glass are fast disappearing in the United States, although in Europe and Asia there is no lack of skilled workers or of handmade glass.

Since the 1960s White House entertaining has become less formal, and dinners are not so elaborate as the 29-course meals favored by the Grants a century ago. The Kennedys introduced round tables seating eight to ten, an arrangement still used today. President Gerald Ford gave the most recent white-tie dinners—for Emperor Hirohito in 1975 and for Queen Elizabeth in 1976. Since then all dinners in the State Dining Room have been black-tie affairs, even the "state dinners"—those given for visiting heads of state or government.

Each new President usually entertains foreign ambassadors at a formal reception early in his term. The justices of the Supreme Court are often invited to a private lunch or dinner with the President, and members of Congress receive invitations to an annual Christmas ball and to a picnic on the lawn.

From Washington to Bush, American Presidents have recognized the role that official entertaining plays in advancing their diplomatic and political goals. Many of the state dinners, levees, receptions, and musicales held in the President's House in the 19th century were meant to show Europeans that the New World had as much culture and refinement as the Old. The shapes and styles of glassware used in the White House at these events varied from the simple to the ornate, but all exemplified, for their time, the height of style.

Some museum and private collections have examples of 19th-century presidential glassware, primarily because of the White House sales that took place until 1902. Lincoln-pattern pieces are most common, but a few pieces in the Jackson pattern are found as well. The Russian-pattern set is rarely seen outside the White House, for Mrs. Roosevelt's dictum that the damaged pieces be destroyed came when that pattern had been in use for less than two decades. The pattern ordered by Franklin and Eleanor Roosevelt was never sold to the public—but since Hawkes offered the same pattern without the insignia, there must be many unengraved sets in private hands. There may be examples of the extensive service ordered by Pierce in private collections, too; perhaps this publication will aid in their recognition.

Collectors of White House china must be wary of reproductions made since the Centennial in 1876. Fortunately, glass collectors do not have to worry about copies. No known reproductions of any White House glassware sets have ever been made for sale as souvenirs.

From time to time glasses with engraved or etched eagles or with versions of the Great Seal turn up in antique shops and at auctions, often identified as glass from the White House. Table glass with an etched version of the Great Seal has been made for the State Department for American embassies since the 1930s. Some of it is American, made by Bryce Brothers and by other firms, and some has come from Europe. None, however, has any connection with the White House. The eagle has always been a popular symbol of the Republic, and its presence on a piece of glass does not imply an association with the President or with his official residence.

*"Your Majesty . . . I take the greatest of pleasure in extending the hospitality of
the United States to you. . . ." As champagne glasses meet, President Gerald Ford
toasts Queen Elizabeth II during the U. S. Bicentennial celebration in 1976.*

Appendix I

For reasons of length and readability, the longest glass inventories are given here and in *Appendix II*. The information immediately following is taken from the "Inventory of the Furniture of the Executive Mansion, December 13, 1869, exclusive of plants in the conservatory." This inventory, in the National Archives, consists of 28 handwritten, unnumbered pages in a bound volume: *Inventory of Public property belonging to the United States, submitted to the House of Representatives, by letter, January 24, 1871. 41st Congress, 3rd session.* Glass entries are on pages 22–23.

Glass, New	*Glass, Old Set*
48 Finger-bowls	48 Wine-glass, coolers
67 Goblets	52 Red finger-bowls
47 Punch-glasses	11 Goblets
42 Champagne glasses	6 Center dishes
47 Claret	10 Salt-cellars, high
47 Hock	10 Salt-cellars, low
45 Wine	10 Celery glasses
24 Liquer	8 Celery glasses, small
6 Claret decanters	36 Water bottles
12 Wine decanters, large	3 Liquer decanters
12 Wine decanters, small	10 Hock decanters
48 Water bottles	7 Claret decanters
6 Celery glasses	4 Wine decanters, large
6 Sugar bowls	2 Wine decanters, small
8 side dishes	48 Wine-glasses, red
3 Center dishes	48 Wine-glasses, white
41 Ice-cream plates	47 Wine-glasses, red border
17 Salt-cellars, frosted	47 Wine-glasses, green

Glass, Old

46 Claret	46 Fine sherry
22 Liquer	40 Champagne
50 Madeira glasses	44 Lemonade
47 Brown sherry	19 Old glasses
36 Pale sherry	

The more complete inventory below was made the following day. It was later included in a report to Congress and is fully cited in note 150.

Miscellaneous glass

6 julep-glasses	12 plain bouquet holders
44 champagne glasses	18 claret glasses
63 sequin glasses	32 finger bowls
47 wine glasses, red	16 plain goblets

Coat-of-arms glass

45 goblets	34 champagne glasses, large
77 sherry glasses	41 champagne glasses, small
57 Madeira glasses	40 punch glasses
45 hock glasses	31 stem sherry glasses
45 finger bowls	39 ice cream plates
6 sugar bowls	10 celery dishes, large
4 celery dishes, medium	5 celery dishes, small
50 champagne glasses	50 hock glasses, green

25 finger bowls	26 ice cream dishes
6 preserve dishes	7 salad dishes
12 decanters	47 goblets
12 decanters with handles	13 decanters
9 decanters, small	2 decanters, pantry
3 custard stands, glass	40 bouquet holders
7 salad stands	49 finger bowls, red
8 preserve dishes	4 salt dishes
101 water bowls	48 champagne
51 punch	35 sherry

The 63 sequin glasses in the inventory are perplexing, for "sequin" has no known meaning in relation to glass. The listing may be a transcription error. The 101 water bowls are probably a mistake. Perhaps "water bottles" was meant, since the individual water carafes from the Jackson, Pierce, and Lincoln services are not otherwise listed. The 8 preserve dishes and 3 custard stands may be the 8 side dishes and 3 center dishes on the list made the previous day.

Appendix II

The following inventory of January 4, 1876, is cited in note 162. The glassware below was in the butler's pantry:

84 water-bottles, cut-glass and plain	6 cut-glass sugar-bowls
100 cut-glass ice-cream plates	20 celery-glasses
68 cut-glass finger-bowls	59 decanters
100 cut-glass goblets	7 glass bowls (large)
96 champagne-glasses, large, cut glass	10 cut-glass bowls (large)
69 liquor-glasses	3 cut-glass, large, flower-tops
130 Madeira-glasses	25 salt-cellers, small
104 green-hock glasses	14 cut-glass preserve-dishes
114 stem-sherry glasses	40 glass bouquet-holders
99 claret-glasses	with silver stands
100 punch-glasses	11 plain bouquet-holders
68 red claret-glasses	47 finger-bowls
46 finger-bowls, plain	38 cordial-glasses
73 glasses	48 small champagne glasses
117 plain claret	35 champagne, large
48 Madeira	27 stem glasses
95 green claret	72 plain goblets
96 Madeira	71 sherry
95 champagne	5 odd sherry
10 julep	12 odd champagne
62 liquor	48 cordial

More glassware was stored in the private dining room:

12 red finger-bowls	13 red claret glasses
16 plain goblets	13 stem-glasses
10 cut-glass champagne-glasses	7 plain claret-glasses
3 plain champagne-glasses	10 plain sherry-glasses

Acknowledgments

This book, like most research efforts, was in some respects a group project in which I was ably assisted by the staff of the Office of the Curator at the White House. Staff members opened their files for my inspection, dug out documents I missed, and checked files at the National Archives for me. I am grateful to William Allman and Lydia Barker, on whose shoulders much of this work fell, and especially to Betty Monkman, whose idea this project was, and who continually offered encouragement. I am also appreciative of the willing assistance of Gary Walters, White House chief usher.

Rex Scouten, curator of the White House; Bernard R. Meyer, executive vice-president of the White House Historical Association; Robert L. Breeden, president of the association's board of directors; and Donald J. Crump, director, offered support along the way, especially when the book grew much longer than I had thought it would be. I hope the result justifies their confidence in me.

At The Corning Museum of Glass, Dwight Lanmon, director, read the first draft of the manuscript and offered the photographic services of the museum. Nicholas Williams made the wonderfully lucid photographs of the glassware. Priscilla Price and Jill Thomas-Clark kept careful records of the photography. Sheila Tshudy spent hours finding obscure references for me through interlibrary loan. I am grateful for all their efforts. At home my husband, Don, taught me how to use his word processor and came to my aid when the machine confounded me. There would be no book without him. My children, Beth and Sam, did without my company on weekends for nearly a year while the book took shape. I appreciate their forbearance.

At the Special Publications Division of the National Geographic Society, Jane R. McGoldrick, editor, and Viviane Silverman, art director and designer, gave the book form, grace, and style. I appreciate both their competence and their patience. Philip B. Silcott, associate director, served as adviser and prudent reviewer. I would like to thank the following staff of the Society for their contributions: Martin G. Anderson, Ross Bankson, Sharon Kocsis Berry, Kathleen M. Cirucci, Richard M. Crum, Jennifer A. Kirkpatrick, Sandra F. Lotterman, and Robert W. Messer.

Margaret Klapthor's *Official White House China: 1789 to the Present* was the model I used in this work, and I am grateful to Margaret for reading the manuscript, for her encouragement, and for the use of her files. I hope this book will be as helpful to collectors as hers has been. Susan Adler at the library of the New-York Historical Society has checked many references for me, saving me several trips to the city. I am also grateful to James Snider of the Hayes Presidential Center and to Kenneth Lyon, both of whom allowed us to photograph pieces of former White House glassware now in their care.

Presidents of the United States and Known Glass Company Suppliers

George Washington	April 30, 1789–March 3, 1797	
John Adams	March 4, 1797–March 3, 1801	
Thomas Jefferson	March 4, 1801–March 3, 1809	
James Madison	March 4, 1809–March 3, 1817	Bakewell, Page and Bakewell
James Monroe	March 4, 1817–March 3, 1825	Bakewell, Page and Bakewell, New England Glass Company
John Q. Adams	March 4, 1825–March 3, 1829	
Andrew Jackson	March 4, 1829–March 3, 1837	Bakewell, Page and Bakewell
Martin Van Buren	March 4, 1837–March 3, 1841	
W. H. Harrison	March 4, 1841–April 4, 1841	
John Tyler	April 4, 1841–March 3, 1845	
James K. Polk	March 4, 1845–March 3, 1849	
Zachary Taylor	March 4, 1849–July 9, 1850	
Millard Fillmore	July 9, 1850–March 3, 1853	
Franklin Pierce	March 4, 1853–March 3, 1857	Haughwout & Dailey
James Buchanan	March 4, 1857–March 3, 1861	
Abraham Lincoln	March 4, 1861–April 15, 1865	Christian Dorflinger, New England Glass Company
Andrew Johnson	April 15, 1865–March 3, 1869	E. V. Haughwout & Company
Ulysses S. Grant	March 4, 1869–March 3, 1877	Hoare & Dailey/Corning Glass Works, Christian Dorflinger
Rutherford B. Hayes	March 4, 1877–March 3, 1881	
James A. Garfield	March 4, 1881–September 19, 1881	
Chester A. Arthur	September 19, 1881–March 3, 1885	
Grover Cleveland	March 4, 1885–March 3, 1889	T. G. Hawkes & Company/Corning Glass Works
Benjamin Harrison	March 4, 1889–March 3, 1893	C. Dorflinger & Sons
Grover Cleveland	March 4, 1893–March 3, 1897	T. G. Hawkes & Company/C. Dorflinger & Sons
William McKinley	March 4, 1897–September 14, 1901	T. G. Hawkes & Company/C. Dorflinger & Sons, Libbey Glass Company
Theodore Roosevelt	September 14, 1901–March 3, 1909	C. Dorflinger & Sons
William H. Taft	March 4, 1909–March 3, 1913	C. Dorflinger & Sons
Woodrow Wilson	March 4, 1913–March 3, 1921	C. Dorflinger & Sons
Warren G. Harding	March 4, 1921–August 2, 1923	Central Glass Works
Calvin Coolidge	August 2, 1923–March 3, 1929	
Herbert Hoover	March 4, 1929–March 3, 1933	Bryce Brothers
Franklin D. Roosevelt	March 4, 1933–April 12, 1945	Bryce Brothers, T. G. Hawkes & Company/Tiffin Glass Company, Libbey Glass Company, Steuben Glass
Harry S. Truman	April 12, 1945–January 20, 1953	T. G. Hawkes & Company
Dwight D. Eisenhower	January 20, 1953–January 20, 1961	T. G. Hawkes & Company
John F. Kennedy	January 20, 1961–November 22, 1963	Morgantown Glass Guild
Lyndon B. Johnson	November 22, 1963–January 20, 1969	
Richard M. Nixon	January 20, 1969–August 9, 1974	Fostoria Glass Company
Gerald R. Ford	August 9, 1974–January 20, 1977	
Jimmy (James E.) Carter	January 20, 1977–January 20, 1981	
Ronald Reagan	January 20, 1981–January 20, 1989	
George Bush	January 20, 1989–	

Notes

Information on Sources

Most of the sources used in producing this book are in the National Archives. MTA indicates "Miscellaneous Treasury Accounts," in Record Group 217 in the Archives—the group into which most of the accounts fall. Record Group 42 is the designation by the Archives for the group that includes the correspondence of the Office of Public Buildings and Grounds (OPBG).

Because the 19th-century descriptions of presidential entertaining are cited in the notes, a bibliography would be redundant. William Seale's two-volume *The President's*

House: A History is the best general description of life at the White House. *The Story of the White House*, by Esther Singleton, and *Official White House China*, by Margaret Brown Klapthor, are invaluable sources for accounts of social customs at the President's mansion. Two other excellent books are *The Living White House*, by Lonnelle Aikman, and *The First Ladies*, also by Margaret Klapthor. The best general works covering the history of the American glass industry are still *American Glass* and *Two Hundred Years of American Glass*, both by George S. and Helen McKearin.

Abbreviations

The following abbreviations will be found in the notes:
LC: Library of Congress
NA: National Archives
    MTA: Miscellaneous Treasury
      Accounts for the President's House,
      Record Group 217
    OPBG: Office of Public Buildings
      and Grounds, Record Group 42
OCWH: Office of the Curator,
    the White House

I. *George Washington to John Quincy Adams*
THE EARLIEST GLASSWARE

1. Henry B. Hoffman, "President Washington's Cherry Street Residence," *New-York Historical Society Quarterly Bulletin* 23 (July 1939): 96.

2. Anne H. Wharton, "Washington's New York Residence," *Lippincott's Monthly Magazine* 43 (1889): 742.

3. Susan Gray Detweiler, *George Washington's Chinaware* (New York: Harry N. Abrams, 1982), 212.

4. *Ibid.*, 4.

5. Helen Harcourt, "The President's New Year Receptions, Then and Now," *Americana*, January 1911, 2.

6. Stephen Decatur, Jr., *Private Affairs of George Washington* (Boston: Houghton Mifflin Company, 1933), 167–68.

7. *Ibid.*

8. *Ibid.*, 260.

9. *Ibid.*, 300.

10. Detweiler, *Washington's Chinaware*, 218.

11. LC. George Washington Papers, vol. 110, *List of Articles, Public and Private*, February or March 1797.

12. Margaret Brown Klapthor, *Official White House China: 1789 to the Present* (Washington: Smithsonian Institution Press, 1975), 27.

13. *Ibid.*

14. OCWH. David Brooks to Maria Mallam Brooks, June 9, 1797.

15. "Joint Committee Appointed to Consider . . . Accommodations of the President of the United States," House of Representatives Report, 6th Cong., 2nd sess., February 27, 1801, 12.

16. Margaret Bayard Smith, *The First Forty Years Of Washington Society,* ed. Gaillard Hunt (New York: Charles Scribner's Sons, 1906), 391–92.

17. Mrs. Harrison Smith [Margaret Bayard Smith], "The President's House Forty Years Ago," *Godey's Lady's Book*, November 1843, 215.

18. NA. MTA. Account 21.304.

19. LC. Thomas Jefferson Papers, vol. 186 (copy, OCWH).

20. Esther Singleton, *The Story of the White House* (New York: The McClure Company, 1907), 1: 42–43.

21. Conover Hunt-Jones, *Dolley and the "great little Madison"* (Washington: American Institute of Architects Foundation, 1977), 22.

22. Lord Francis Jeffrey, "Journal of a Trip To the United States in 1813" (typescript, OCWH).

23. *Ibid.*

24. NA. MTA. Account 29.494, voucher 6.

25. *Ibid.*, voucher 8.

26. *Ibid.*

27. *Ibid.*, voucher 9.

28. *Ibid.*, voucher 7.

29. *Ibid.*, voucher 23.

30. *Ibid.*, voucher 14.

31. *Ibid.*, voucher 40.

32. William Seale, *The President's House: A History* (Washington: White House Historical Association, 1987), 134–35.

33. NA. MTA. Account 28.634, voucher 2, no. 20.

34. *Ibid.*, voucher 1, no. 23.

35. *Ibid.*, voucher 1, no. 28.

36. *Ibid.*, voucher 2, no. 29.

37. *Ibid.*, voucher 3, no. 31.

38. *Ibid.*, voucher 22.

39. LC. James Madison Papers, Benjamin Bakewell to James Madison, February 19, 1816 (courtesy Susan Detweiler).

40. The author is indebted to Conover Hunt-Jones for this information from her files.

41. Long Island Historical Society (now the Brooklyn Historical Society). Unnumbered files.

42. C. G. Sloan & Co., Public Auction, April 26–28, 1985, no. 1938, 107.

43. Klapthor, *White House China*, 40.

44. NA. MTA. Account 43.754, voucher 86.

45. Henry Bradshaw Fearon, *Sketches of America. A Narrative of a Journey of Five*

Thousand Miles Through the Eastern and Western States of America. . . . (London: Longman, Hurst, Rees, Orme, and Brown, 1818), 204.

46. *Providence Gazette and Moral, Political, and Commercial Register,* November 29, 1817, 3.

47. *Pittsburgh Gazette,* November 10, 1818, 3. This story has been incorrectly cited in a number of articles as appearing in the *Pittsburgh Mercury,* a rival paper, which in fact was not published on that particular date.

48. Lowell Innes, *Pittsburgh Glass, 1797–1891: A History and Guide for Collectors* (Boston: Houghton Mifflin Company, 1976), 112.

49. "A. JARDEL. GLASS ENGRAVER Has just opened his Store . . . where he will neatly, and at a moderate price, engrave and execute everything that may be wished. . . ." *Pittsburgh Mercury,* April 3, 1818.

50. *Niles* (Baltimore, Md.) *Weekly Register,* December 11, 1819.

51. Kenneth M. Wilson, *New England Glass and Glassmaking* (New York: Thomas Y. Crowell and Co., 1972), 244.

52. Singleton, *White House Story,* 1: 148–49.

53. NA. MTA. Account 43.754, voucher 34.

54. Klapthor, *White House China,* 45–46.

55. "Inventory of Furniture in the President's House, taken the 24th day of March, 1825," House of Representatives Report No. 2, 19th Cong., 1st sess., December 7, 1825, 131.

56. NA. MTA. Account 51.873, voucher 10.

57. Mrs. E. F. Ellett, *Court Circles of the Republic* (Philadelphia: Philadelphia Publishing Company, 1872), 131, 133.

58. Lonnelle Aikman, *The Living White House* (Washington: The White House Historical Association, rev. ed. 1987), 43.

59. Klapthor, *White House China,* 49.

60. *Ibid.*

II. *Andrew Jackson to James Buchanan*
THE JACKSON AND PIERCE SERVICES

61. Klapthor, *White House China,* 51.

62. Edwin A. Miles, "The First People's Inaugural—1829," *Tennessee Historical Quarterly* 37 (Fall 1978): 305.

63. Smith, *First Forty Years,* 295.

64. *Charleston* (S.C.) *Courier,* March 13, 1829.

65. Klapthor, *White House China,* 52.

66. NA. MTA. Account 61.369, voucher 54.

67. "Notes and Queries," *Western Pennsylvania Historical Magazine* 6, no. 3 (July 1923): 191–92.

68. The Hermitage. Jackson Papers, Henry Baldwin to Andrew Jackson, April 11, 1828.

69. Quoted in Hortense F. Sicard, "Glassmaker to Two Presidents," *The Magazine Antiques* 25, no. 2 (February 1934): 56.

70. *Connecticut Courant,* August 11, 1829.

71. Jackson Papers, Jackson accounts, February 1832.

72. "Documents—1834: Letter of Robert Caldwell," *American Historical Review* 27 (January 1922): 273–74.

73. NA. MTA. Account 61.369, voucher 54.

74. NA. MTA. Account 70.467. List of articles sold by P. Mauro & Sons, December 5, 1833.

75. NA. MTA. Account 70.467, voucher 4.

76. Klapthor, *White House China,* 60.

77. "Furniture of the President's House," House of Representatives Report No. 552, 27th Cong., 2nd sess., April 1, 1842, 1–58.

78. Jessie Benton Fremont, *Souvenirs of My Time* (Boston: D. Lothrop Company, 1887), 94.

79. NA. MTA. Account 75.138, voucher 28.

80. *Ibid.,* voucher 21.

81. House Report 552, 38, 40.

82. NA. MTA. Account 81.944, voucher 1.

83. Singleton, *White House Story,* 1: 256.

84. Miss [Eliza] Leslie, *The House Book or, A Manual of Domestic Economy* (Philadelphia: Henry Carey Baird, 1840), 254.

85. LC. Martin Van Buren Papers, invoice, Davenport Company to Martin Van Buren, June 25, 1839 (courtesy Martin Van Buren National Historic Site).

86. NA. MTA. Account 87.086, orders to May 28, 1842; NA. MTA. Account 93.470, voucher 28, June 1842–April 1845.

87. Ellet, *Court Circles,* 345–46.

88. Seale, *President's House,* 266, 268.

89. NA. MTA. Account 93.470, voucher 2.

90. *Ibid.,* voucher 3.

91. Ebenezer Collamore is not to be confused with Davis Collamore, another china and glass retailer in New York City from 1840 until the end of the century.

92. NA. MTA. Account 96.137, November 12, 1846.

93. Tennessee State Library and Archives. Tennessee Historical Society Collection, James K. Polk Papers, Joanna Rucker to "Bet" [Elizabeth C. Prince], October 17, 1845.

94. *Ibid.,* April 7, 1846.

95. Connecticut Historical Society. Manuscript diary of Mrs. J. E. Dixon.

96. NA. OPBG. Letters Received, Ignatius Mudd to Col. William W. Bliss, January 1, 1849.

97. NA. MTA. Account 101.316, May 30, 1849.

98. NA. MTA. Account 102.509, December 27, 1849.

99. NA. MTA. Account 103.151, voucher 4.

100. *Ibid.*

101. NA. MTA. Account 105.580, voucher 3.

102. *Ibid.*

103. *Ibid.*, voucher 2.

104. NA. MTA. Account 107.778, voucher 6.

105. *Ibid.*, voucher 10.

106. *Ibid.*, voucher 16.

107. Klapthor, *White House China*, 73.

108. *Ibid.*, 74.

109. Ellet, *Court Circles*, 460.

110. Klapthor, *White House China*, 74–75.

111. *Official Catalogue of the New-York Exhibition of the Industry of All Nations* (New York: 1853), 80.

112. There are two Haughwout billheads in the Landauer Collection of New-York Historical Society. The one dated 1858 lists "Brooklyn Cut Glass"; the one dated 1867 does not. Bills in 1861 and 1866 in the National Archives show "Brooklyn Cut Glass." The firm moved to Corning in 1868.

113. NA. MTA. Account 113.810, voucher 4.

114. Leslie, *The House-Book,* 258.

115. OCWH. Abby Gunn Baker notebook.

116. NA. MTA. Account 116.018, voucher 14.

117. NA. MTA. Account 113.810, voucher 3.

118. Mrs. Roger A. [Sarah A.] Pryor, *Reminiscences of Peace and War* (New York: 1904), 51.

119. Klapthor, *White House China,* 74.

120. NA. MTA. Account 130.243, voucher 12.

121. *Ibid.*, voucher 9.

122. NA. MTA. Account 134.023, voucher 31.

123. NA. OPBG. Accounts Received, voucher 13, November 18, December 2, 1858.

124. NA. MTA. Account 134.023, voucher 19.

III. *Abraham Lincoln to Grover Cleveland*
THE LINCOLN SERVICE

125. Elizabeth Todd Grimsley, "Six Months in the White House," *Illinois State Historical Society Journal* 19, nos. 3–4 (October 1926–January 1927): 50.

126. Klapthor, *White House China,* 81.

127. It has been previously assumed that Zimaudy was a Washington retailer. But a search of contemporary Washington business directories and the 1860 Census has failed to discover either his name or business location. A search of Brooklyn and Manhattan directories was also fruitless.

128. NA. MTA. Account 141.158, no voucher. Although the dealer has been listed as Zimandy in previous articles, the name is clearly Zimaudy on his invoice.

129. Maureen O'Brien Quimby and Jean Woolens Fernald, "A Matter of Taste and Elegance: Admiral Samuel Francis Du Pont and the Decorative Arts," *Winterthur Portfolio* 21, nos. 2–3 (Summer–Autumn 1986): 131.

130. Grimsley, "Six Months in the White House," 62.

131. Frank H. Swan, *Portland Glass Company* (Providence: The Roger Williams Press, 1939), 6–7.

132. *Corning* (N.Y.) *Daily Journal,* Special Trade Edition, September 4, 1895.

133. Edna M. Colman, *Seventy-five Years of White House Gossip* (Garden City: Doubleday, Page & Company, 1925), 289.

134. *Frank Leslie's Illustrated Newspaper,* New York, February 22, 1862.

135. *New York Herald,* February 5, 1862.

136. NA. MTA. Account 157.178, voucher 60.

137. *Ibid.*, voucher 9.

138. OCWH. Abby Gunn Baker Papers, William Dorflinger to Mrs. Wm. H. Baker, April 17, 1914.

139. NA. MTA. Account 157.178, voucher 24.

140. NA. OPBG. *Inventory taken at President's House,* Letters Received, no. 3713, May 26, 1865.

141. Mary Clemmer Ames, *Ten Years in Washington* (Hartford: A. D. Worthington & Co., 1874), 240.

142. NA. OPBG. Letters Sent, B. B. French to E. V. Haughwout, July 10, 1865.

143. NA. MTA. Account 157.178, voucher 18.

144. Quimby and Fernald, "A Matter of Taste," 131.

145. NA. OPBG. *Inventory of furniture &c in the President's House,* Letters Received, no. 3813, February 28, 1867.

146. Seale, *President's House,* 446.

147. Ames, *Ten Years,* 250.

148. NA. MTA. Account 173.118, voucher 7.

149. Klapthor, *White House China,* 90.

150. "Inventory of the Furniture of the Executive Mansion, December 14, 1869. . . . " *Inventory of Public Property About the Capitol,* House of Representatives Document No. 45, 42nd Cong., 3rd sess., 33–35.

151. NA. MTA. Account 180.754, voucher 5, December 6, 1870.

152. *Corning* (N.Y.) *Journal,* December 22, 1870.

153. Ames, *Ten Years,* 172.

154. Edward Winslow Martin, *Behind the Scenes in Washington* (New York: Continental Publishing Co., 1873), 380–82.

155. *Corning* (N.Y.) *Journal,* August 1, 1873.

156. *Ibid.*, October 31, 1873.

157. *Oakland* (Calif.) *Daily Herald,* January 5, 1874.

158. NA. MTA. Account 192.686, voucher 90.

159. NA. MTA. Account 192.686, voucher 81.

160. John Quentin Feller, "Identifying President and Mrs. Grant's Dorflinger Glass," *The Glass Club Bulletin,* no. 156 (Fall 1988): 3–8.

161. Seale, *President's House,* 482.

162. "Inventory of public property in the President's House," [ca. December 8, 1875], *Inventory of Public Property,* House of Representatives Document No. 39, 44th Cong., 1st sess., January 4, 1876, 25–26.

163. *New York Daily Graphic,* April 25, 1877.

164. Singleton, *White House Story,* 2: 154.

165. Hayes Presidential Center, Fremont, Ohio. Hayes family scrapbook of the White House years.

166. Ben: Perley Poore. *Perley's Reminiscences of Sixty Years in the National Metropolis* (Philadelphia: Hubbard Brothers, 1886), 349–350.

167. Emily Apt Greer, *First Lady: The Life of Lucy Webb Hayes* (Fremont, Ohio: Rutherford B. Hayes Presidential Center, 1984), 154.

168. Klapthor, *White House China,* 97–115.

169. Hayes family scrapbook, *passim.*

170. Society for the Preservation of New England Antiquities. Thomas L. Casey Papers, "List of Articles purchased for Refurnishing Executive Mansion" (copy, OCWH.)

171. Abby G. Baker, "The White House Collection of Presidential Ware," *The Century Magazine* 6, no. 6 (October 1908): 830.

172. NA. OPBG. Accounts Received, voucher 2, June 29, 1881.

173. *Washington Post,* April 15, 1882.

174. Klapthor, *White House China,* 122.

175. OCWH. Manuscript, "List of Articles, in serviceable condition, in the Executive Mansion, May 13, 1882."

176. NA. MTA. Account 233.637, voucher 45.

177. Seale, *President's House,* 547.

178. Poore, *Perley's Reminiscences,* 459, 462.

179. NA. OPBG. Accounts Received, voucher 49, November 21, 1882.

180. *Ibid.,* voucher 59, October 17 and November 26, 1884.

181. NA. OPBG. Letters Received, M. W. Beveridge to Col. John Wilson, July 28, 1885.

182. NA. OPBG. Letters Received, Thomas G. Hawkes to Col. John Wilson, July 28, 1885.

183. NA. OPBG. Letters Sent, Col. John Wilson to T. G. Hawkes, July 29, 1885.

184. *Crockery & Glass Journal* 22, no. 10 (September 3, 1885): 28.

185. Dorothy Daniel, *Cut and Engraved Glass, 1771–1905* (New York: M. Barrows & Co., 1951), 184.

186. Poore, *Perley's Reminiscences,* 499.

187. John Quentin Feller, "Identifying President and Mrs. Lincoln's Dorflinger Glass," *The Glass Club Bulletin,* no. 155 (Spring 1988): 8.

188. Seale, *President's House,* 573.

IV. *Benjamin Harrison to Woodrow Wilson*
THE RUSSIAN PATTERN

189. Corning Museum of Glass, Rakow Library. Richard Briggs to Thomas Hawkes, June 17, 1885. Quoted in T. G. Hawkes & Co., *Hawkes Cut Glass* (Corning, ca. 1897), 27.

190. Daniel, *Cut and Engraved Glass,* 184.

191. NA. OPBG. Letters Sent, Col. John M. Wilson to T. G. Hawkes, May 6, 1889.

192. NA. OPBG. Letters Sent, Col. Oswald Ernst to M. W. Beveridge, June 17, 1891.

193. Estelle Sinclair Farrar and Jane Shadel Spillman, *The Complete Cut & Engraved Glass of Corning* (New York: Crown Publishers, Inc., and The Corning Museum of Glass, 1979), 141.

194. NA. MTA. Account 287.852, voucher 74.

195. George Evans. *Visitors' Companion at Our Nations Capital* (Philadelphia, 1892), 79.

196. OCWH. Unidentified newspaper clipping, June 1891.

197. NA. MTA. Accounts Received, voucher 27, June 25, 1894.

198. NA. MTA. Accounts Received, voucher 7, November 5, 1894.

199. NA. OPBG. Letters Sent, John M. Wilson to M. W. Beveridge, April 9, 1896.

200. *Ibid.,* April 29, 1896.

201. *Hawkes Cut Glass,* 26.

202. NA. MTA. Accounts Received, voucher 10, June 26, 1896.

203. NA. OPBG. Letters Sent, Theodore A. Bingham to M. W. Beveridge, September 14, 1897.

204. *Corning* (N.Y.) *Daily Journal,* August 4, 1898.

205. NA. OPBG. Letters Sent, Theodore A. Bingham to Estate of M. W. Beveridge, July 22, 1898.

206. Carl U. Fauster, *Libbey Glass Since 1818: Pictorial History and Collector's Guide* (Toledo: Len Beach Press, 1979), 80.

207. NA. OPBG. Letters Sent, Theodore A. Bingham to Dulin & Martin, Feb. 27, 1901.

208. NA. General Accounting Office, 22485, voucher 36, June 24, 1901.

209. "Inventory of public property in the Executive Mansion, June 30, 1901," Appendix A, *Annual Report of the Chief of Engineers for 1901,* Appendix DDD (Washington, D. C.: Government Printing Office, 1901), 3747–48.

210. W. G., "The White House as a Social Centre," *Harper's Bazar* [now *Bazaar*], February 1908, 160–61.

211. NA. OPBG. Letters Received, Van Heusen Charles Co. to Miss T. S. Hagner, December 1, 1902.

212. *Ibid.,* March 24, 1902.

213. Philadelphia Museum of Art Archives. Edwin A. Barber to W. F. Dorflinger, May 16, 1903. I am indebted to Miriam Mucha for drawing this correspondence to my attention.

214. Philadelphia Museum of Art Archives. W. F. Dorflinger to Edwin A. Barber, May 19, 1903.

215. *Ibid.,* June 24, 1903.

216. "Inventory of public property in the Executive Mansion, June 30, 1903,"

Appendix A, *Annual Report of the Chief of Engineers for 1903,* Appendix EEE (Washington, D. C.: Government Printing Office, 1903), 2602–05, 2626–29.

217. NA. MTA. Account 41795, voucher 73, March 31, 1906.

218. NA. OPBG. Letters Sent, Col. Bromwell to Galt & Bros., Harris & Shafer Co., Dulin & Martin Co., Charles R. Edmonston, June 7, 1906.

219. *Corning* (N.Y.) *Daily Journal,* September 19, 1906.

220. NA. OPBG. Letters Sent, Col. Bromwell to Galt & Bros., November 10, 1906.

221. Archibald Butt, *The Letters of Archie Butt,* ed. Lawrence F. Abbott (Garden City: Doubleday, Page & Company, 1924), 19.

222. *Ibid.,* 160.

223. *Ibid.,* 246.

224. *Ibid.,* 245.

225. *Ibid.,* 237–38.

226. *Ibid.,* 365.

227. NA. General Accounting Office, no. 13176, voucher 23, February 9, 1910; General Accounting Office, no. 23900, voucher 54, February 19, 1912. Information from Dorflinger records, courtesy John Quentin Feller.

228. Seale, *President's House,* 792.

229. NA. OPBG. Letters Received, Tiffany & Co. to Col. W. W. Harts, June 27, 1917.

230. *Ibid.,* September 17, 1917.

231. NA. OPBG. Letters Sent, Col. W. W. Harts to Mitchell Kendall, September 24, 1917.

232. NA. OPBG. Letters Received, Tiffany & Co. to Col. W. W. Harts, October 15, 1911.

233. NA. OPBG. Letters Sent, Col. W. W. Harts to Dulin & Martin, July 12, 1917.

234. NA. General Accounting Office, no. 46383, voucher 100; General Accounting Office, no. 51956, vouchers 121 and 122.

V. *Warren G. Harding to the Present*
20TH-CENTURY GLASS

235. *Crockery and Glass Journal,* May 26, 1921, 16.

236. Farrar and Spillman, *Complete Cut & Engraved Glass of Corning,* 209.

237. *Focus on Corning: The Crystal City of the World* (Corning: Chamber of Commerce, 1948).

238. Seale, *President's House,* 842.

239. Farrar and Spillman, *Complete Cut & Engraved Glass of Corning,* 209.

240. Seale, *President's House,* 858.

241. Klapthor, *White House China,* 154.

242. Vylla Poe Wilson, "The Place of Wine on White House Menus," *The Washington Post Magazine,* March 11, 1934, 3.

243. OCWH. Howard Ker to Mrs. William B. Umstead, June 15, 1939.

244. Henrietta Nesbitt, *White House Diary* (Garden City: Doubleday & Co., 1948), 198–99.

245. OCWH. Correspondence from Hawkes, April 3, 1939.

246. Records of all of these orders are in the Office of the Curator, the White House.

247. OCWH. Records.

248. *Ibid.*

249. OCWH. William P. Graham to J. Bernard West, April 11, 1958.

250. OCWH. Invoice, Morgantown Glassware Guild, May 31, 1961.

251. OCWH. Mrs. John F. Kennedy to Mrs. Henry Parrish, July 16, 1962.

Composition

Composition for WHITE HOUSE GLASSWARE by the Typographic section of National Geographic Production Services, Pre-Press Division. Type set in Times Roman and Vivaldi. Film preparation, printing, and binding by Peak Printers Inc., Cheverly, Maryland.

Interpretation of the U. S. coat of arms,
an engraved insignia on a 20th-century goblet
symbolizes the ideals, traditions,
and history of our 200-year-old Republic.

Interpretation of the U.S. coat of arms,
an engraved insignia on a 20th-century goblet
symbolizes the ideals, traditions,
and history of our 200-year-old Republic.